LEARN TO
Find Inner
Peace

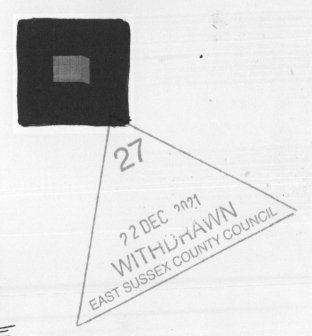

LEARN TO
Find Inner Peace

discover your true self
manage your anxieties and emotions
think well, feel well

MIKE GEORGE

WATKINS PUBLISHING
LONDON

Learn to Find Inner Peace
Mike George

This edition first published in the United Kingdom and Ireland in 2010 by
Watkins Publishing, an imprint of Duncan Baird Publishers Ltd
Sixth Floor, Castle House
75–76 Wells Street
London W1T 3QH

Conceived, created and designed by Duncan Baird Publishers

Editorial Consultant: Clifford Bishop
Managing Editor: Judy Barratt
Editor: Karen Sullivan
Designers: Jan Harte and Meredith Harte
Commissioned artwork: Marion Deuchars, Joelle Nelson and Aud Van Ryn

British Library Cataloguing-in-Publication Data:
A CIP record for this book is available from the British Library

ISBN: 978-1-907486-21-0

1 3 5 7 9 10 8 6 4 2

Typeset in Bodoni and Liberty
Colour reproduction by Scanhouse, Malaysia
Printed in Hong Kong by Imago

Publisher's note:
The information in this book is not intended as a substitute for professional
medical advice and treatment. If you are pregnant or are suffering from any
medical conditions or health problems, it is recommended that you consult a
medical professional before following any of the advice or practice suggested in
this book. Duncan Baird Publishers, or any other persons who have been involved
in working on this publication, cannot accept responsibility for any injuries or
damage incurred as a result of following the information, exercises or therapeutic
techniques contained in this book.

DEDICATION

*With boundless gratitude to the Comforter of Hearts,
to the Dadis, whose radiant spirits are lighthouses
to the world, and to the Brahma Kumaris World
Spiritual University for the most profound education
in caring for the soul.*

contents

introduction

Almost 30 years ago I found myself in an open-eyed meditation with over a hundred people on Mount Abu in north-west India. At around 6 pm on a calm, sun-kissed evening, I had the most profound spiritual experience. For what was probably only 20 seconds – although it felt like forever – I was engulfed in a brilliant white light which I could only describe as pure spirit. All sense of the world dissolved, including my body. As this light filled my consciousness, I was aware of being at its source, whose presence was both familiar and tremendously beautiful. In this subtle encounter I felt a soundless voice convey three things, for which these words are totally inadequate – *welcome home, your search is over* and *I love you*. There was an overwhelming feeling of meeting my oldest and dearest friend after a thousand years apart. I can never forget the intensity of the love that poured into my being.

This experience altered the course of my life. Since then the exploration of spirit and spiritual development has been at the forefront of all that I do. What changed me deeply was not just a reunion with a being I came to consider the source of spirit, but the awakening of a deep insight into our true nature. I realized that it is not that I have a soul or spirit somewhere in my body, or in me, but that I *am* a soul, I *am* spirit! As I continued to master the art of meditation, the fruits of my efforts were both humbling and sweet. I began to experience my own eternity and a deep sense of our imperishable existence as spiritual beings. The gradual liberation from fear and the flowering of a peacefulness from deep within was the beginning of a growing awareness of the "inner beauty" of spirit.

While much has been said and written about spiritual truth, it seems that few people have been empowered by the reality of the experience. This is clear from the two main clues that demonstrate the poverty of spirit in the world today. First, there is an abundance of fear, evidenced by the amount of conflict and violence in our world. And secondly, everyone is searching, although they might not be consciously aware of this. Behind our consumption of the movie, the music and the exotic meal, behind our striving for position,

power, pay and possession, behind our desire for attention, acceptance and approval, every human soul is searching for the three most important experiences of its existence – love in our relationships, happiness in everyday experience, and peace in our fluctuating and peaceless natures. But the search is almost entirely externalized, which is why most of us miss the spiritual paradox of our times – we already have what we seek. When we experience ourselves as we really are, soul not body, spirit not matter, we wake up to our innate spiritual qualities. Love, happiness and peace never leave us; *we* leave *them* when we lose our awareness of our own spiritual identity. These qualities of spirit are the source of all real wealth and true joy, and they are the greatest gifts we can give to each other.

The insights and exercises in this book are designed to help you focus your search in the right direction: inwards, to the real you, the spiritual you; upwards, to reconnect with the source of spirit, a relationship with the One who awaits patiently, lovingly, to guide you home; and finally outwards, to share the rediscovery of your inner peace with the world.

Mike George

the universal path

The route toward spiritual awareness is a journey, the most important journey of our life; but it is not our lifetime's journey.

It has often been stated that wisdom comes with time. Our physical powers wane as our mental powers wax: we exchange youthful vigour for maturity of thought. Hence the idea of the wise old person, offering his or her teachings to the young, who continue, of course, unheedingly to pursue their follies. But this notion is a dangerous fallacy when applied to our quest for spiritual awareness. It is dangerous because it implies that we may neglect matters of the spirit until our later years. According to this view, even in middle age, say in our 40s or 50s, we do not have to worry too much if we are still carrying around with us some of our youthful attachments – our ambition, our drive, our tendency to rush headlong into projects. Yet, in fact, if awareness is withheld from us until the time of sunset revelations, we will have wasted some of our potential. It can never be too late, but given the inestimable rewards of spiritual awareness, given above all that this is the only satisfactory way to live, why not make a start immediately? This book is a gentle wake-up call to do so.

Some of the associations of a journey are highly appropriate to the spiritual quest. The aim is to travel far from what has become habitual to us. There may be long periods en route when we do not seem to be making progress, when the landscape does not appear to change. We may feel tired (we are on foot, of course) and wish that we had never started. We may miss our home comforts from time to time. We will cover the ground more effectively if we choose to travel light.

Yet the spiritual quest is different in fundamental ways from any geographical quest. It differs above all in the following characteristic: that we are looking for something that was ours all along, something easily and instantly accessible, that we could rediscover at any moment. We tend to think of the pilgrim's long, arduous trek, whose very hardships are the guarantee of spiritual authentication. However, this is a conceptual pitfall, popularized by the attitude of *no pain, no gain*, by which effortless achievement is regarded with suspicion. Better to think that the spirit's journey, your journey, is without distance – more to do with being than doing, staying than going, as the discoveries we need to make are only a second away. The only

obstacles are our own negative thoughts, such as *I can't*, or *This is difficult*, or *I'll always be like this*. As you work through this book, reflecting on its themes and trying its exercises, you may suddenly, at any time, feel an inward shift – a flash of insight that you cannot describe. You may not be able to hold it for very long, for on the spiritual journey you will arrive at your destination many times, then slip back to an earlier stage of progress. Then, one day, you will realize that you have been in the right place for some time, and you will know that you are there forever; you will feel the peace and love that guarantee this; you still have much to learn and to give, but you know that this is your destiny.

This book is thematically arranged around the following topics: learning to make sense of life (pp. 14–39); an introduction to spiritual growth, planned around the seasons (pp. 40–49); learning to find true self-esteem (pp. 50–65); liberating the self from temptations and distractions (pp. 66–79); the spiritual implications of nature, art and music (pp. 80–97); learning to find peace (pp. 98–117); learning to find love (pp. 118–139); learning to deal with life's difficulties (pp. 140–151). The conclusion (pp. 150–3) describes how spiritual awareness is the basis of character and maturity. The following pages (pp. 12–13) provide a concise glossary of terms that are used throughout the book. Each essay in the book is designed to be instructive in its own right, but also forms part of a kaleidoscopic program of developing spiritual awareness.

the language of the spirit

Many of us have an instinctive understanding of spirit, a sense of our own life force and being. We may be sensitive to the energy of others. But how do we even begin to verbalize the intangible?

Throughout this book, certain key concepts recur. The intention here is to introduce them, as if setting out the *dramatis personae* of a play. Alongside each term are notes that an actor might make if he or she were working on a particular role. In other words, these are not comprehensive definitions, but suggestive prompts that help to characterize the leading elements in the spirit's drama. These words may help us to express what it means to be on the spiritual journey.

Spirit: Life energy, eternal, indestructible. The soul. A unique, conscious entity that inhabits and animates the human form. The vital principle. We speak of spirit or the spirit, and the meaning is the same. Equates with self, power and love, because all these qualities, like spirit itself, are indivisible. I do not have a spirit – I *am* spirit.

Spiritual awareness: Self-knowledge and acceptance. Living by the spirit rather than the ego. Overcoming attachments. Understanding that the cycle of birth, life and death is not the ultimate reality or our ultimate destiny. Being aware of and communing with the source (godhead) in the highest spiritual relationship. Becoming aware of the spirit is a process of awakening – a kind of rediscovery.

Ego: Powerful when spirit/self loses its true self-identity. When we identify ourselves with things outside ourselves, like position, possessions, beliefs, we experience fear and anxiety at the possibility of damage or loss, and therefore "suffer" from ego. In many ways, egotism is the opposite of spirituality.

Love: At its deepest, the natural outpouring of benevolent feelings upon all people. Flow of positive energy from the spirit. Deep feeling of solicitude – of being one with everyone and everything around us, while retaining awareness of the individual self.

Karma: Law of returns. The energy we give comes back to us. If we do wrong, it comes back as negative energy. If we give love, we are enriched immeasurably. In Eastern thought it is believed that one's state in this life is the result of physical and mental actions in past incarnations and that present action can determine one's destiny in future incarnations. A natural, impersonal law of moral cause and effect.

self, world and spirit

The movement of our spirit in the world is like a beautifully choreographed dance. The possibilities for finding new steps to match the changing tempo of the music are endless, but our spirit – the core of the self – remains changeless, whatever the mood or pace of the music.

Our bodies are incidental to our identity, which is why the modern cults of beauty and style should be treated with scepticism. Neither do the various roles we play in life, nor the chance circumstances that befall us, define our essence. We are, quite simply, spirit, and recognizing this will lead us to question certain basic misconceptions we might have about our relationship with other people, with time, with change, and with all the world's phenomena as perceived by our senses. An understanding of spirit also brings us to call into question the faculty of reason, which in the Western world has been elevated by the scientific empirical tradition far above its proper status, and the validity of the emotions, which serve only the ego.

If we look inside ourselves we will rediscover the reality of spirit, and if we take this self-understanding as our compass in life, we will learn to live more creatively, more lovingly and more peacefully. We will have faith in our intuitions and be able always to act confidently and with a clear conscience, in the knowledge of our accumulating spiritual wealth.

chaos and meaning

Does life have meaning? This is a question that students and philosophers have considered for centuries. Yet the answer must derive not from intellectual argument but from intuitive experience. Once we have awoken to our own spiritual truth, all philosophical questions become irrelevant. The meaning of life lies in the reality of our experience as spiritual beings.

For many of us, at the deepest level, the world seems incomprehensible and therefore full of fear. What organizing principle makes sense of the arbitrary phenomena that surround us and impact

upon us, the world of accidents both natural and social? Amid such chaos, what clear purpose is served by our lives? How wonderful it would be if the purpose we serve turned out to be the very thing that makes sense of the world's randomness – its seething convolutions of change and chance.

As a starting-point for engaging with these mind-teasing issues, step back from daily concerns and try to think of the world as a vast spider's web network of cause and effect, which follow highly complex but identifiable laws of existence. If we think like this, we will see that events that may seem arbitrary are really the playing out of universal necessities: what can happen will happen. To struggle against chance, to waste the imagination by wishing that things were otherwise, is a pointless misuse of spiritual energy.

To be spiritually aware is to make sense of the world. This is because spirit is the organizing principle, the centre of light that reveals the true concentric meaning of what otherwise might seem to be chaos. Just as a mirror performs no function until someone looks into it, so the world makes no sense until observed and understood – in a flash of experience – by spirit. When interpreted by ego, the world may seem chaotic and meaningless, because it refuses to conform to the ego's wishes. When interpreted by spirit, the world is inevitable, and our life is an unfolding of energy within the circumstances that outwardly impinge upon us. By expending energy, we bring all the important changes within our grasp: the rest is acceptance of a world that makes sense in spiritual terms.

exercise 1

making sense of seashells

Imagine a long beach with shells of about six different kinds strewn along it. The first shell will be a surprise to us – a gift offered by chance. Further along the beach, we might come across a second shell of a different type – another surprise. As we find more shells we realize that they are a characteristic of the beach. We find that there are six kinds, some more common than others. We become aware of a pattern in what originally seemed to be a sequence of random encounters – we find meaning in apparent chaos. This narrative can be used as the basis for a meditative exercise.

the pattern of blessings

Look back at some of the blessings in your life perhaps encounters with inspiring people, or moving experiences of the landscape. Trace the pattern these blessings have made, a pattern that continues as you progress on life's journey. Visualize the next inspiring person you will meet: what will he or she be like? Or the next wonderful landscape: will it be wooded or treeless, gently rolling or mountainous? Meditate on these imagined blessings for a few minutes. Close your session by thinking about the positive patterns that your life has revealed to you so far.

perception and reality

In our daily experience of the material world we often respond habitually to what we see. For example, we think of a blue sky as a backdrop to the landscape, a two-dimensional field. We may know that the sky is blue because it is the colour created by light of the longest wavelength – the only wavelength that is not filtered out from sunlight by our atmosphere. We acknowledge the truth of this scientific insight without allowing it to affect our responses. Perception becomes habitual.

In many spiritual traditions the inability to see clearly is an integral part of being human. In Hinduism our perception of the material world is illusion, or *maya*. The cosmos is in fact a dream of Brahma, the creator god. In this belief, all things are one: our rational categories are fabrications of the human mind, without ultimate reality.

Appearances cannot be trusted, for two principal reasons. First, we are physiologically constructed to believe in what we see, yet the most important element in life – spirit – cannot be apprehended by any of the senses, only by intuition. Furthermore, the ego, with its obscure, self-seeking agenda, and its wishes, hopes, fears and attachments, often casts a distorting veil around reality.

In Western philosophy much has been made of subjectivism – the idea that the material world exists only when someone is perceiving it through the medium of their senses. When we look away from the apple tree in our garden, that apple tree ceases to exist. According to some Christian philosophers, we ourselves exist because we are the objects of continuous divine scrutiny. There are some accidental parallels here with the notion of *maya*. However, this whole notion of subjectivism can be turned on its head. It is the unseen that is the ultimate reality. Whatever pleasure we may take in the variety of the world's forms, our most profound joy comes from the apprehension of the invisible – the pure source of love within ourselves.

The spirit offers fulfilment beyond the spectrum of all that the senses can encompass.

exercise 2

windows on wonder

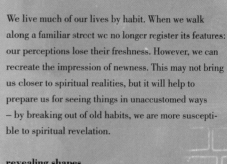

We live much of our lives by habit. When we walk along a familiar street we no longer register its features: our perceptions lose their freshness. However, we can recreate the impression of newness. This may not bring us closer to spiritual realities, but it will help to prepare us for seeing things in unaccustomed ways – by breaking out of old habits, we are more susceptible to spiritual revelation.

revealing shapes
Take a familiar object such as a teapot or desklamp and try to see it as pure object, without any functional implications. Absorb yourself in its colour and shape. What is it made of? Does it have any intrinsic beauty? How would it appear if you had no inkling of its use?

new perspectives
On a dry, sunny day, lie on your back in a park and view the world from this new perspective. Passers-by will be upside down, and nearby flowers will be seen from the side. Contemplate the idea that an adjustment of angle does not change the reality of what you see. You may, however, see things as you have never seen them before, and taking time to view things from a fresh perspective offers you rare moments of wonder.

the four pillars

Visualize four strong white pillars, holding up a table laden with a luscious feast. If one of the pillars gives way, the table will wobble and may even collapse. If one of the pillars is cracked, or shorter than the others, there can be no balance. In a similar way the true life of the spirit is balanced by four strong and equally important pillars, called Gyan, Yoga, Dharna and Seva.

Gyan

Gyan is knowledge and study, and lifts us toward spiritual fluency. The basis for study is knowledge of oneself, a supreme understanding of ourselves as spirit, an indestructible point of spiritual energy.

We are peace and we have an eternal and personal relationship with the source. These are the parts that make us whole.

Study is alive and ever-changing. We examine how our thoughts are created, how our memories work to sustain or to bind us, how we make our decisions. We also watch our habits of thinking. Our thoughts predispose us to view everything in a particular way, but even long-standing patterns can be changed through awareness. From reflection – the ultimate basis of study – comes understanding of ourselves and of others, allowing the spirit time to gather insights, and to accept the realizations that spring from them.

Yoga

Yoga is meditation, a discipline of mastering the mind, the intellect and sanskars, the impressions gathered from action over time. We use meditation not to stop or cancel thoughts but to create the right kind of thoughts.

We are soul and light. We embody spiritual energy. We radiate peace and love. In the process of meditation we restore our true self-awareness, bringing us back to the radiant light of our original and true being.

Meditation turns on an inner light that allows us to perceive our thoughts, actions and world more clearly. Intellect becomes sharper and we can dive deeper. Habit and ego slip away.

Through this, we gain insight, which is a new direct view into ourselves as spirit. We acquire a valuable new perspective on life and a deep sense of knowing that is not based on formal learning. We gain insight by practising mindfulness (see p. 86). As we observe ourselves, we begin to see more clearly. A moment of insight is a personal experience – the gift of meditation.

Dharna

Dharna is the assimilation of the divine virtues, which are always within us and can be expressed whenever we choose – by an act of conscious remembrance. From a state of inner calm, we can destroy ego and its attachments, and annihilate anger, greed, lust and other destructive emotions, and we can realize wisdom, courage, truth, peace, love, patience and acceptance We can also, when circumstances require it, extend forgiveness toward others – as well as toward ourselves.

Becoming attentive to moments of goodness in our lives rekindles the fire of self-awareness and provides us with the sparks we need to continue on the path to light. In the peace of the evening, consider the day that has passed. Which virtues were given room to soar?

Seva

Seva is service, an acknowledgment that whatever we have that we hold to be most precious is to be shared. The highest form of giving is to pass on to others what we have learned and gained through our knowledge of ourselves as spirit. On our continuing spiritual journey, we awaken those around us so that they can share the light.

To serve others' needs before we serve our own is the highest form of leadership. The "servant-leaders' " deepest acts of *seva* are those that nurture and sustain the spiritual growth and well-being of others. When this level of spiritual service is authentic it seeks neither reward nor recognition in return, making us all potential leaders.

It is upon these four essential pillars that we build a truly spiritual lifestyle. Each pillar needs to be strengthened equally to achieve symmetry and to support our natural spiritual purpose. Both their balance and their strength are the basis for our own continuous enlightenment, as well as our expanding capacity to nourish the minds and hearts of others.

creativity and spirit

The surprising reason why many people fail to find fulfilment in their lives is because they are plagiarists. They adopt the pre-packaged images that surround them – on TV, in the movies and in print. So prolifically are these images generated that they offer the illusion of a wealth of options. In the end the mind becomes addicted to the ready-made patterns with which society presents it, and gives up on the possibility of truly evolving. This is a tragedy, because it runs counter to the mind's responsibility for directing its own evolution. Every thought is an act of creation. If it is not ignored or buried, it will have an impact in the world. Many people live as if the future were written in stone, or the result of events beyond control. Both approaches ignore the visionary within us all, that part of the mind capable of conceiving its own destiny and bringing that destiny about. We think of creative people as those who have inherited a talent or achieved creative skills through long practice. If we paint or write or garden, we may be modest about our success. Yet, the greatest creative workshop of all is the human mind that all of us possess. We all have the capacity to be utterly original in our thinking, and we can fulfil this potential on a daily basis. Part of the secret of creativity is being relaxed and confident.

Think of a relationship with a good friend. In a responsive, relaxed friendship, there will be creativity in the dialogue you share, the plans you make and the stories you concoct to entertain each other. This kind of calm and comfortable rapport inspires imagination, which is a gift of spirit. By working toward spiritual awareness, we develop relaxed self-confidence that enables our creativity to shine. In its light we release the inestimable gift of our best thoughts, which are no less precious for not being consciously framed, as art is, to survive the moment.

Make visible what,
without you,
might perhaps never
have been seen.

.

Robert Bresson (b. 1907)

exercise 3

fresh perspectives

Perhaps the two most pervasive enemies of creativity are self-doubt and laziness. It is safer and easier to keep quiet and let ourselves be entertained than it is to speak up and work toward refining our own message. Here are some ways to help you create your own way of looking at the world.

thinking in images

Get into the habit of thinking visually, to stretch your imagination. For example, when thinking about a friend, ask yourself whether he or she has the qualities of a particular animal – perhaps a lion (majestic, self-possessed), a gazelle (fleet-footed, graceful) or a dolphin (playful, sociable). By thinking in visual terms, you will often be able to seize upon insights that reason and language are unable to articulate.

stream of consciousness

Tap into your creativity by keeping a daily "stream-of-consciousness" journal, beginning as soon as you wake up. Write things down exactly as they occur to you, without editing or censoring them. Write as quickly as you can, to shortcircuit your internal critic. What you write does not have to make sense. One day, as you re-read what you have written, sense will surface.

reason and intuition

Intuition is the natural wisdom of the spirit. Reason, left to its own devices, would argue away the existence of spirit. Through reason, with materialistic science as its ally, we arrive at a perception of the self as a complex neuro-electrical charge, a state of being composed of trillions of impulses buzzing away within the nervous system. This view makes us all a prisoner of the material world, a ghost that the machine itself has created.

However, the reality is that we are free, that we have only to push open the door of our cell, with the gentlest of touches, to be able to walk in the pure light of being. The faculty that alerts us to this freedom is intuition, often called the sixth sense. This is a good description, because, like the five other senses, intuition is an instant source of information. But, it is more than a device for providing us with raw data. It is our innate quality of knowingness, of assessing the truth of a situation in a moment – like a clear river of wisdom flowing into consciousness from spirit.

Attribution of omnipotence to reason is as bad a piece of idolatry as is worship of stock and stone believing it to be God.

.

Mahatma Gandhi
(1869–1948)

Intuition tells us that the self must exist as a primary entity. To think otherwise would reduce existence to a vast emptiness and deprive us of a compass by which to steer through life. Yet instinctively we know that we do have such a compass, the self, and that the self is non-material – even though we recognize that there are aspects of our personality influenced by external factors. Through intuition, we perceive our vitality, our individuality.

So what are the status and role of reason? If perception of the spirit is intuitive, does that make reason an enemy of spiritual awareness? Not entirely. The 17th-century English philosopher Thomas Hobbes believed that reason's function was as a servant to our emotions. This is a cynical view, of course, suggesting that we are all prey to self-deception, although Hobbes was certainly right in assuming that reason is often misused. A more positive interpretation of reason's function is that it is a harmonizing, controlling force rather than a creative one. We need it at an

everday level to negotiate the choices we have to make and trace cause forward to effect, effect back to cause. Yet reason must be subject to the higher court of intuition, which prevents it from leading us in the wrong direction or taking a wrong turn altogether.

An example of intuition at work is the oper-ation of conscience. When we behave badly, counter to spiritual truth, the voice of con-science alerts us to our error. We may ignore that voice, recruiting reason as the ally of the ego to justify our actions. Yet the troubling intuitive rebuke of conscience will continue to make its remonstrations. We have the choice of suppressing

this advice or of altering our course and repairing the wrong. Only if we choose the second of these options is our spiritual peace restored.

If we think of ourselves as essentially spiritual beings, we will see that intuition connects us with the core of our being in a way that reason does not. And whereas reason can often be a barrier between people, intuition joins them. Once we tune into someone else's sixth sense, rapport is almost instant. But when we try to describe this connection in words, the instruments of reason, it takes wing – like a delicate butterfly we catch sight of for a moment before it is carried out of sight by the breeze.

emotion and feeling

Although the words "emotion" and "feeling" are often used interchangeably, there is a fundamental distinction between them. One way of understanding the difference is the analogy of sight: emotions are blind, feelings perceive.

Emotions, which stem from the lower, physical part of our natures, are out of our control and are often destructive. We talk of having a "fit" of passion, of being in the "grip" of fear, or being "beside ourselves" with rage. An emotion visits us like a storm that comes from nowhere and often leaves us shaken by the experience. After the visitation we look back and can see that we have behaved unlike ourselves. Our true spiritual nature has been momentarily taken hostage.

And the hostage-taker is the ego, who has unleashed his hounds of emotion with characteristic effect.

It may be easy for us to recognize that emotions such as anger and jealousy, which make us feel bad, are negative forces that we need to

> *The recesses of feeling ... are the only places in the world in which we catch real fact in the making, and directly perceive how events happen.*
>
> •
>
> William James
> (1842–1910)

learn to control. We may, however, have more difficulty in seeing that emotions such as passion, triumph and pride, which make us feel good, are also destructive. The truth is that all emotions are the result of attachments, which pull us away from our spiritual foundations toward a world of egotistical responses. In the process we are uprooted, the self becomes weakened, and we lose some of our true identity.

Emotions can also be contagious. If we try to reach out to someone who is consumed by emotion, we can be truly helpful only if we avoid drawing their emotion into our own being. Because emotion is negative energy, we risk endangering our own positive life-force, our own sense of calm, which is the basis of all that we have to offer.

Love is often regarded as the supreme emotion. In fact, true love overcomes its emotional roots and begins to draw strength and character from the spirit. "Love" in the initial stages of a relationship is more likely to signify desire, attachment and dependency.

Emotion is agitation, feeling is perception. In feeling, our mind reaches out and uses its intuitive skill to test for value. If we are spiritually aware, we are able to feel clearly, as if we are opening our eyes to let in light. Feeling is the warm, sensitive route to the truth, midway between the heat of emotion and the coldness of intellect.

This may seem difficult, but it may be clarified by an example. Remember when you met someone for the first time. Your intellect told you that you were acquainting yourself with a set of biographical circumstances, or a set of opinions. Emotionally, you may have experienced anything from dislike to physical attraction. But what did you feel? What exchange of energies took place? Every encounter leaves an intangible impression, an indelible feeling that represents two spirits meeting. Feelings are the antennae that register the significance of our exchanges.

To avoid drowning in emotions, we need to take charge of them, to rise above the swell into a higher realm of feeling. If we cultivate spiritual awareness, we can make this possible. Because we are truly spiritual, we are sealed against the corrosive effects of the emotions, which dissolve in the acid of their own irrelevance. The extent to which we feel immune to the emotions is a litmus test of our spiritual strength.

putting time in perspective

Time is a human invention – a device of consciousness that enables us to believe that the flow of life itself is measurable. We cannot be content simply to live: we feel the compulsion to capture and quantify our past and our future, using clocks and watches to graduate even the most metaphysical aspect of our reality.

Many of us cannot function properly without being able to know the precise clock time, accurately or approximately, at any given instant. The problem is that this acute sensitivity to the time makes the clock our master, hampering our ability to live in the moment. Some advanced mystics can, through meditation, suspend the flow of time through their consciousness and in doing so experience the purity of the absolute present. In a more modest way we can take our own steps to undo the tyranny of time, and in the process come closer to inner peace.

Part of the skill of this is to extend our sense of time's artificiality by a series of imaginative contemplations. At two o'clock this afternoon you may be reading this book, while half way across the world a friend, on vacation, at precisely the same moment (but at an entirely different time), may be enraptured by a concert of music. In listening to that music, he experiences each passage as it happens, although there is no doubt that the value of the music lies in the whole experience. It is as if a wave of life – the composer's life – were flowing through him. If he is appreciating the music, he is unlikely to look at his watch. When the performance is over, the music does not die, or cease to exist, but neither do we rack our memories to experience it again. There are many suggestive parallels here with the human lifetime. Each moment, each passage is relished for what it is, yet the sense of the whole is all-important. Time is the concert hall in which life's music is performed. The music of spirit is beyond measure, and exists as beauty and truth independently of its players.

exercise 4

the clockless day

If you ever get the chance to enjoy a completely clockless day, seize it with relish. Obviously, this is easiest to arrange at weekends or on vacation. You may need to enlist the cooperation of your family, even if they are continuing to live by clock time. The idea is to follow natural rhythms of hunger, thirst, sleeping and waking. A clockless day is not necessarily one without tasks – the tasks simply have no time limit.

1. The night before your chosen day, remove all clocks and watches from sight. Turn off your alarm clock. Make sure that you have suitable provisions in the home so that you are not dependent on store opening times.

2. Your day begins when you awaken naturally – either with the sunrise or when you have had the right amount of sleep. Obey your body's rhythms. There may be several things you have to do. Decide which ones you will aim to do before lunch. Busy yourself on them one after another until you feel it is time to eat. Do not worry if you do not complete everything you planned to do. As you undertake each activity, focus on its quality. Between tasks, try to concentrate your whole attention on whatever you do. Remember that this day is devoted to quality, not to measurement or achievement.

change

At the dawn of the first millennium, the Roman poet Ovid wrote about transience in words with which it would be hard to disagree: "All things change, nothing is extinguished ... . There is nothing in the whole world that is permanent. Everything flows onwards; all things are brought into being with a changing nature; the ages themselves glide by in constant movement."

Change pulls in many directions. In the outside world a part of us fears change, for it intrudes on the comforts of habit. Another part of us is drawn to change, for it stimulates and excites. In different people these parts are mixed in different proportions. We also think about change in terms of our own attitudes and behaviour, even our own personalities. We all feel dissatisfied with ourselves, and believe that we can and will change; yet still we steer through life by what we know of ourselves, by anticipating how we will react – for example, avoiding certain situations because we know that we will not respond well to them.

This is the unenlightened view of change – as a problem. As we look at these matters from a spiritual per-

spective, the picture begins to appear more complex and yet more reassuring, although none the less challenging.

Change, according to the spiritual view, is the essence of the material world, and we cannot resist it. As the Greek philosopher Heraclitus said, "No one bathes in the same river twice." If we try to resist physical change, we will create tensions and torments within ourselves when things do not go according to plan. The only way to pre-empt such tensions is to understand that the unchanging spirit passes through waves of change like a spaceship travelling through the asteroid belt, and that this is natural and inevitable. The asteroids are not inimical to spirit – they are neutral – but they can cause us to stop or change our route, and they will make the ride bumpy.

Some changes, far from being obstacles, will turn out to be highly enjoyable. It is pleasant for the senses to be stimulated by new sensations, such as those of travel, or the intellect by unfamiliar ideas. But when our liking for change turns to addiction, there is a shift within ourselves, as we begin to be

centred in the accidental, the material, rather than in the spiritual. This shift leaves us unprepared to deal with the next wave of undesirable change – the next asteroid belt. We have become passive recipients, allowing the world to give to us – and, in turn, we readily take. However, we can derive much more fulfilment by giving to the world, as it changes around us. This is the essence of spiritual awareness.

If spirit, which equates to self, is changeless, is the idea of "self-improvement" a perversion? The answer is that we cannot make ourselves what we are not. But we are certainly more than we

think ourselves to be, and finding this "more" is the true purpose of our quest. Success will come from unlearning as much as from learning.

We do not need to become more self-assertive, extrovert or creative. There are ways to achieve these characteristics, but they are not the ways of the spirit. Our primary aim is to discover who we are. This is the movement from the belief that we are spirit in identity and spiritual in nature, to the actual experience of spiritual qualities. Once we have intuited who we are, positive changes will flow from us naturally and abundantly, like light from a distant star.

self and other people

Imagine you are drifting down a river, sometimes swimming, sometimes just floating. Your body does not absorb the water that surrounds you, although it feels the water's touch. So it is with our spiritual selves, as we swim alongside others in the flow of life. We are alert to the lives of other people, but we are not attuned to them. We may empathize with some of them, but they cannot deflect us from our destiny.

Peace, love, truth, power and happiness – these are the core qualities of the spirit. When we awaken to the reality of these qualities within ourselves, we channel them outward and transform our relationships with others by offering them the gift of our energy. All our relationships involve energy exchange, but the most profound form of giving is that which is unconditional: we measure neither what we give out nor what we receive. Giving is the breath of the spirit.

To feel such transformative power, we first need to still any emotional turbulence that others might stir up in our minds. For example, we may feel anxiety upon entering a room full of people or a crowded train carriage, or even joining a small gathering for lunch or dinner. What we fear are the emotions that people can arouse in us (when this happens it is fear of fear, or chronic anxiety, that is really at work). It may be that we see ourselves through others' eyes rather than in the self-generating light of our own spirit. In the face of such anxieties, affirmations can help enormously.

Repeat the following affirmation (inwardly or aloud) from time to time until you absorb the deep truth of the message: *I am my touchstone of truth and value; no-one is of greater worth than I; people cannot touch my true self unless I wish them to, however unexpected the things they do or say.*

If we are spiritually self-aware, we recognize that just as others cannot change us, so, conversely, we cannot change others, nor will we have any need or desire to do so. The more we try to control people, the less influence we actually have over them, and the more disturbance we cause

> *The ultimate lesson all of us have to learn is unconditional love, which includes not only others but ourselves as well.*
>
> ·
>
> Elisabeth Kubler-Ross
> (b. 1926)

within ourselves from the frustration of trying to alter the unalterable.

Human beings cannot truly and happily live in isolation. We may choose a relatively solitary path, but still it is our relationships with others that will largely define the quality of our lives. However much we value our freedom, we will seek to give our energy to others, which is indeed the highest use of our freedom. We share our energy and our peace, in a spontaneous act of giving that equally rewards others – the recipients – and ourselves, the donor.

A state of true self-awareness removes the egotistical need for us to judge, attack, criticize or control others. Any fear that others might be capable of arousing in us dissolves in the knowledge that we are one with them, even if they themselves are not aware of this.

The health of all our relationships with others, from the most to the least intimate, depends upon our relationship with our own self – our awareness of spirit. When we cultivate that awareness the garden we inhabit with others will bloom of its own accord.

limitless energy

There is a common tendency to talk about "nourishing the soul", when in fact it is the soul that nourishes all other aspects of life. Our real goal on any spiritual journey is not to "do things" to the soul in order to develop or change it, but rather to stop doing the things that suppress its flowering. The task is not to gain more power, or more energy, but to avoid dissipating what we already have. Caring for the soul means caring for the self, and all the energy we need lies within us, in limitless abundance.

The energy that flows within and around us all is volatile. There are people who give and people who take. If we lack spiritual strength, we will be susceptible to the negative energy of others. For example, if a friend is angry with us, and we don't understand why, we may feel something akin to guilt, even though we believe in our own innocence.

At the opposite extreme are exceptional people who radiate so much positive energy that they have the power to heal, by touching, or simply by coming close to someone who is ill. Everyone who becomes spiritually aware will be able to radiate a beneficial energy that is not exactly healing, in this physical sense, but nevertheless has a strong transforming power. In the presence of such wholeness, other people may feel their own spiritual weaknesses opening up, as if calling out to be strengthened.

Consider friends whose sparkling energy uplifts you – they give without knowing it, and they have the ability to energize those around them. Conversely, you will know other people whose negative energies would drain or exhaust you if you allowed it.

When we give out energy in our dealings with people, we do so without expecting to receive anything from them in return – at least directly (though we will derive it ultimately through karma; see p. 130). Because energy is self-renewing, we will not be drained by what we give: on the contrary, we will be refreshed.

exercise 5

detecting the life-force

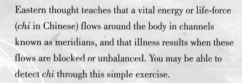

Eastern thought teaches that a vital energy or life-force (*chi* in Chinese) flows around the body in channels known as meridians, and that illness results when these flows are blocked or unbalanced. You may be able to detect *chi* through this simple exercise.

1. Stand with your feet parallel, shoulders' width apart, head erect, knees slightly bent, arms hanging loosely.

2. Place your hands in front of your lower abdomen, palms facing each other. Imagine your hands are encircling a ball of energy. Hold this position for 2 minutes. Move your hands slowly outward until they are shoulders' width apart. Imagine the ball of energy expanding as you do so. Hold for 1 minute.

3. Imagine the ball of energy contracting as you move your hands toward each other again. Repeat this movement several times. Your fingers may tingle, or your hands may feel warmer. You may also feel a sensation within your abdomen, a crucial energy centre.

4. Contract the ball of energy until it fits inside the abdomen. Feel the energy compress to a bright point. Let go of your hands and shake them.

source of the spirit

According to Hindu belief, *atman* (the Sanskrit word for self or individual spirit) is of the same essence as, but distinct from, *brahman* (the source of spirit). One of many Westerners inspired by this idea was the 19th-century American poet Walt Whitman, who believed that true knowledge comes through union with the Self in its universal sense. At such moments of union (which Whitman called "merge"), we see with enhanced clarity and can read infinite lessons in common things. Our essential and original divinity of the individual spirit implies the equality of all and the universal responsibility we share for loving each other.

The idea of a transcendent spirit, or godhead, is present in most religions. Commonly this universal spirit is symbolized as light. It is also described as the source, a kind of inexhaustible spiritual reservoir to which we are all connected. This sense of derivation brings in the idea of parenthood – spiritually, we are the offspring of the source.

Try to hold these three ideas in your mind simultaneously: light, source, parent. But bear in mind too that no image or analogy is ever going to be able even to come close to conveying the true quality of the source, which to use an old-fashioned theological word is "ineffable" – too great or intense to be rendered in words.

In the same way that the physical source of life is the sun, the spiritual source is the divine, the eternal, the all-encompassing. We can recognize the reality of this within our own spirit with total conviction, but we cannot confirm that reality through the evidence of the senses or through the power of reason. Mystics have testified to their direct contact with the ineffable in language that is often powerful and strange; and people who have undergone near-death experiences have often described a rushing toward a light at the end of a tunnel or an encounter with a blaze of light that radiates unconditional love and acceptance. But if we wish to have a truer sense of the source,

exercise 6

the ultimate reunion

This visualization helps us to experience how infinitely privileged and beloved we all are in our relationship with the source. Find a quiet place and sit comfortably.

1. Gather your thoughts. You are a pure spirit that has travelled far and is about to make the final leg of the journey home. Centre yourself in the middle of your forehead just above and behind the eyes. Imagine your "subtle body" of light rise from the chair, leaving your solid body behind. Feel yourself rise, moving easily through the ceiling and up, high into the sky. Enjoy the silent freedom of a bird on the wing.

2. Ahead, you see space in all its majesty approaching. In a split-second your subtle body becomes a tiny point of shimmering white light: like a comet you race past a thousand galaxies. Then you slow down and enter a field of warm, golden light. Like a quilt of softest down, it enfolds you. You are silent and at peace.

3. You become aware of the glowing core, full of love, inviting you to come close. You feel recognized as a special being. The purity of the love courses through your heart and heals a thousand wounds. You decide you will stay here to enjoy this silent, loving reunion.

it is more fruitful to take a step inward, to the spirit, than to set too much store by the reported experiences of others.

Enter into yourself and inhabit your belief in the source as though it were a wonderful, beautiful mantle – a cloak of indescribable colours. The change you experience as you begin to look at the source from this perspective, from inside, will be argument enough for transcendence.

The heart of spiritual awareness is the reawakening of our relationship with the source. Our relationships on earth are horizontal and progress within limits. Our connection with the source of the spirit is the transcendent, vertical relationship that gives the deepest meaning to life, like the axis around which our world spins. Spiritual awareness is a moving current of energy that carries everything in the direction of higher evolution.

Why do we lose awareness of the supreme source? Mainly because we are enticed by body-consciousness. Like children who go adventuring in the world, we get lost and then cry in panic

I am smaller than the minutest atom, likewise greater than the greatest. I am the whole, the diversified-multicoloured-lovely-strange universe. I am the ancient One, the Lord.
I am the Being-of-God. I am the very state of divine beatitude.

.

Hindu text

– we realize that we have ventured too far from parental love and safety.

Many people believe in God because they are attached to a belief system. They literally "hold" beliefs, hanging on to the dogmas and rituals of religion out of fear or habit rather than love (which keeps fear at bay). This dependence on systems and rules can prevent some people from truly connecting with the source. Purely intellectual belief has little, if any, transformative energy. One indicator that belief can be an attachment rather than an experience is the intolerance that we often find expressed toward people who believe in a different God.

When people tell us that the divine is everywhere, present in everything, yet requiring no obligations of us, we are witnessing a kind of spiritual draft-dodging. The obligations on us to live by the spirit, in love, openness and trust, are in fact profound; and so are the corresponding rewards. If we retrain ourselves to open up to the spirit from whom we came and to whom we will return, we will feel the rightness of this relationship, and we will also feel its joy.

The depth and profundity of spirit are symbolized by white light – a simple, pure beam that draws together every colour under the sun. White light is as invisible to us as the air that we breathe. Yet we can see it when it is separated into its constituent colours in a prism or in a rainbow. In a similar way, we can be directly aware of the source when it is refracted through the prism of our intuitive experience. Spirit has no beginning and no end. It is within us all, and always has been. As a reminder of this eternal relationship, try suspending a crystal prism in front of a window in order to bring rainbow colours into the room. The dancing hues of light will be a personal spiritual symbol. The following visualization is based on the image of rainbow light as a way of coming closer to spiritual reality. It is designed to take you toward the idea of a personal spiritual relationship with the source, and help you to rediscover that friendship.

Find a room where you will not be disturbed for ten minutes. Sit in a comfortable

chair. Take a few deep breaths, close your eyes and clear your mind of distractions. Imagine pure white light filtering through a window and washing over your closed eyes. Feel its warmth and light penetrating your body. The source of spirit is radiating pure white light through the window that is your life, directly into your being. Feel the warmth of love, the light of wisdom, penetrate your inner self. When your mind is full of white light, imagine it separating into the colours of a rainbow. Each hue is a different aspect of your relationship with the source. The red ray is the creative energy you receive from the One. The orange band is the gift of spiritual power: your invulnerability. The yellow ray is the ray of the child, bearing the gift of purity and innocence. The green ray is the relationship of the father to the child, and its gift of self-respect. The blue ray is the gift of friendship, and offers complete devotion. The indigo ray is the peace that fills your heart. The violet ray is the mother, and carries the gifts of sensitivity and caring. Contemplate your spiritual gifts from the One, and reply with silent love.

seasons of the spirit

The passage of the seasons through the year offers a leisurely timetable and symbolic framework for us to begin to think about the spirit, to understand its reality and to live by its eternal truth. In this chapter, we trace a series of thoughts, meditations and spiritual exercises, through each of the seasons from spring to winter.

There are several advantages to working within this seasonal context. First, in becoming aware of nature's cycle, we move away from artifice – clock time, the working week, the ever-increasing toll of birthdays, the long spells of expectancy between vacations. We are able to settle down to a more natural rhythm in our lives.

Secondly, we learn the art of patience. We must not expect to be able to take a crash course in spirituality: the harder we strive for inner peace, the less likely it is that we will gain it. Instead, we must make changes by re-opening ourselves to revelation, and we can do so across the spectrum of the seasons – ever-changing and inspiring. Over a year we will have plenty of time to open ourselves up to self-revelation. What follows is not a structured program, but a suggestive prospectus. The sleeping bud of spiritual awareness could flower within us at any time: it blooms whenever we make ourselves available to its gifts.

spring

Spring or early summer is the perfect time to begin a year's program of spiritual awakening. The full sequence would be: spring (recognizing the miracle of nature through mindful observation and quiet contemplation); summer (developing awareness of the spirit and its implications); autumn (reflections on change and decay); winter (renunciation and taking stock of profound truths).

One reason to attune your spiritual education to the seasons in this way is to deliberately slow down your rate of development – to put a brake, as it were, on spiritual ambitions. Haste is always contrary to the spirit's own rhythms – and patience is a supreme virtue of the spiritually adept.

An excellent starting-point is the season of growth, because this is the time to observe infinitesimal changes in nature – the first stirrings of renewal that can be measured on a daily basis, provided that the mind is unclouded by anxieties and distractions.

*In my new robe
this spring morning –
someone else.*

Basho
1644–94

Accurate observation is both the cause and the consequence of heightened perception; and heightened perception in turn goes hand in hand with an unclouded mind. Or, to put this idea in a less circular fashion, noticing the telling signs of spring will help to lift us above the mundane preoccupations of an unrelaxed, unspiritual approach to life.

Leaf and flower buds that appear overnight are the advance guard of mature natural beauty – promises of an astonishing unfolding of perfection. This "foundation course" of our year's spiritual program should be based on simple contemplation of the details. If we accumulate such impressions in our minds, the beauty of nature will be revealed gradually, from within us – there is no need for us to force this realization. Simply allow the particulars of nature to show its sheer variety and ingenuity – like buoyant objects

that are released from their moorings on the bottom of a lake and come into view as they rise to the surface.

A meditation mandala, made up from the stages of spring as they appear in sequence, can be created over several weeks to help us attune our perceptions. For example, as soon as you notice the first spring bulbs coming through, draw simplified, diagrammatic versions of these at each of the points of a pentagram plotted with the help of a ruler and protractor. Then, when you see a certain kind of leaf unfolding, you might add simplified drawings of this leaf to your mandala, filling in the gaps symmetrically to build up a composite image.

Once you have completed your spiritual diagram, set aside some time when you know that you will not be disturbed so that you can meditate on the mandala. You might imagine that its centre is your spirit, the point from which all your thoughts and actions grow. Just as the leaf-shapes reach outward from the centre, so does your goodness reach out from the spirit into the world around you.

summer

Summer is plenitude – a limitless feast for the senses. The warmth of sun on skin; foliage and flowers in abundance; invisible tracks of flower and herb scents; birds and insects obeying their urgent appetites; the flavours of nature's garden. Two of these sensual dimensions – sight and sound – offer natural subjects for meditation.

Each symmetrical flower is a *yantra* – a universal geometrical symbol of the wholeness of the authentic self, an image that speaks directly to the unconscious. The mind can use such a flower as a focus for meditation. First, sit comfortably near the flower. Then look closely at the flower so that it fills your whole attention. See it as pure shapes and colours. Try to empty your mind of all other concerns, and let the flower enter your consciousness as pure perception. A seasoned meditator might say that the flower is experienced as an aspect of his or her own inner

potential. As you meditate, let this truth gently float on your mind. The reality is simple: if we are successful at letting go of all the distractions that normally flit across our consciousness, we can become pure perception, pure mind, pure spirit. Try to shut out the background buzz of summer and experience this inward purity – if only for a few minutes. But don't strive too hard, or compete with yourself. Meditating on a flower should be as natural for a human being as landing on a flower and sipping its nectar is for a bee.

There is in fact a symbolic reason why a flower should be used in meditation: for its combination of male (stamens) and female (pistils) elements. The *sri yantra* of Hinduism, a set of superimposed triangles converging on a point, follows a similar principle: the triangles are Shiva and Shakti, the divine male and female forces whose union brings into being the levels of the world as we perceive it.

exercise 7

the power of light

The sun may be thought of as a giving eye. It makes biological life possible on this Earth. Like the enlightened spirit, it is pure energy, giving itself absolutely – taking is not in its nature. Use this exercise to begin to think more deeply about correspondences between the sun and spirit.

1. The sun at noon blazes down onto our world. Visualize its light pouring down upon us all (never look at the real sun – you could seriously damage your eyes). In your mind, imagine the sun as a vast ball of light.

2. Think of what scientists tell us about the sun: the temperature at its heart is 27 million °F (15 million °C). This heat is simply unimaginable. Relax your rational thought and imagine spiritual energy, which is similarly impossible to visualize, flowing into the point of light at the centre of yourself – the point that is spirit. Bathe in the realization of your infinite spiritual power.

3. As a "cooling down" exercise, consider how we can't look at the sun without harming our eyes. Anyone who gazed upon the Greek god Zeus in his true form would be burned to ashes. Spirit is all-powerful. We cannot see spirit, only feel its all-giving reality within us.

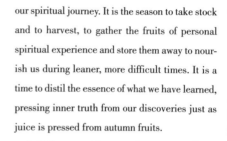

autumn

Autumn makes us aware of the passing year. Unenlightened minds will feel sorrow at the loss of summer, the onset of short, cold days. Ripeness itself – life at its height of fruitfulness, on the very cusp of decay – is seen by the Romantics as inherently poignant. The most basic spiritual exercise for autumn is to rid ourselves of such pseudo-poetic melancholy. True spiritual awareness has no room for regret. The passage of time is no reason for sorrow. When the past streams behind us (or appears to do so, at the experiential level), it must not be allowed to accumulate in some receptacle of regretfulness, alongside failed dreams. If indeed we are carrying such a receptacle around, it can only impede our journey.

Autumn is a good time to think about such matters, and to free ourselves of artificial burdens that will clog our spiritual progress like a carpet of sodden, rotting leaves clinging to our ankles. Nevertheless, we can find in autumn some suggestive metaphors for the development of spirit within the framework of our spiritual journey. It is the season to take stock and to harvest, to gather the fruits of personal spiritual experience and store them away to nourish us during leaner, more difficult times. It is a time to distil the essence of what we have learned, pressing inner truth from our discoveries just as juice is pressed from autumn fruits.

In 19th-century Germany there was a tradition of philosophers taking long walks through the woods to sort out their thoughts: the university of Heidelberg, for example, has a Philosopher's Way along the forested hillside high above the town. Map out your own walk, ideally through woodland, and take time to contemplate the paradoxes of autumn, which relate to a view of time as organic and endless. A fruit scatters the seeds of new life as it rots. The cycle of life and death is not a parabolic rise and fall, but an endlessly recurring wave, in which all living things participate. Our own spiritual development depends on destruction – the abandonment of corrosive, egotistical thinking, so that love can grow in its place. Feel the cold of the coming winter in the winds that scatter the leaves as you walk – biting winds that promise as much as the warm breezes of spring.

exercise 8

fruits of promise

The following year's growth is already contained within autumn's fruits. Although all around us we may see signs of vegetable decay, quiet reflection will make us aware of how that fits into the eternal rhythms of life as a whole. The following meditation on this theme uses an actual fruit transformed into a mandala.

1. Collect some of autumn's fruits from the park or from your garden – horse chestnuts or apples, for example. Select one and cut it in half down the centre with a sharp knife.

2. Take one of the halves and arrange it where you can see it clearly. Usually, some kind of symmetrical pattern will be revealed, although it does not matter if the cross-section is not too regular. This is your mandala for meditation and contemplation.

3. Meditate on the fruit. For about 5 minutes, working from the inside out to the skin, contemplate pure pattern and colour. Then, meditate on the sources of life within the fruit. Imagine the seeds sprouting into new life the following year, after a winter of dormancy. Imagine life itself as a constant through endless cycles of time.

winter

By stripping away illusory comforts, luxuries and distractions, winter presents us with a spiritual challenge. It is natural for us to focus inwardly at this time – to confront our home situation, our relationships with others, the path that we have set for our life's journey. What better season could there be to ensure that we have done enough work on ourselves during the preceding calendar year, that we have been sufficiently thorough in stripping away illusions and props and exposing the deepest realities? The skeletal branches of bare trees, stark under a winter sky, offer a visual reminder of the process that we must go through to arrive at uncompromising spiritual understanding.

A tale of King Arthur and his court tells in symbolic form of the renunciation that the questing spirit must undergo. At a New Year's feast, a giant Green Man charges into the court. He challenges any knight to chop off his head, on condition that he be allowed to return the stroke in a year and a day's time. Gawain accepts the challenge. The giant picks up his own head and rides away. Almost a year later Sir Gawain, riding to the Green Chapel to honour his pledge, takes lodging in a forest. His host proposes that he and Gawain exchange anything they each receive during the knight's sojourn. For three days, the man goes hunting and brings his game home to Gawain. Meanwhile, his wife tries to seduce Gawain, giving him on the first day one kiss; on the second, two kisses; and on the third, three kisses – as well as a life-protecting green belt. The knight tells his host about the kisses, but is silent about the belt. On the fourth day he faces the giant. Later, when the Green Man wields his axe, he merely scratches the knight's neck. "That cut was for the belt," he explains. The Green Man is really another knight, who has been testing the honour of the Round Table. He is also Gawain's host. Gawain rides home with this mild rebuke for lack of self-denial. Arthur commands all his knights to wear green belts henceforth.

*In the depth of winter
I finally learned that
there was in me an
invincible summer.*

.

Albert Camus
(1913–1960)

*In every winter's heart
there is a quivering
spring.*

.

Kahlil Gibran
(1883–1931)

During our wintertime self-examination, it is worth asking ourselves what our own green belt might be – the indulgence that we are most reluctant to give up. We may not be able to renounce this prop yet, but this is, at the very least, a horizon for which we can aim.

In the cold depths of winter, the flame of the hearth or a candle is an appropriate symbol of continuing life, the eternal stillness of spirit clothed in the flux of the material world. As a personal ritual, take the opportunity that winter offers to gaze deep into the core of the flame. The comfort of winter is not in the flame's warmth, nor in its blaze of cheering colour: it is in the eternal reality of spirit.

Against the symbol of the hearth, we might place the contrasting symbol of the snowflake. A perfectly symmetrical mandala, the snowflake melts on contact with most surfaces. There could be no more truthful image of the transience of earthly life, and the importance of experiences that take us beyond the physical.

the inner temple

The forgotten spirit is constantly searching: for identity, self-worth and truth, among other things. "Who am I?" is one of the fundamental questions we need to ask ourselves if we are to re-discover inner peace. We may not immediately define the answer, but we can begin, initially, to move toward self-knowledge by recognizing what we are not. We are not our bodies and we are not essentially any of our roles in life – partner, friend, sportsplayer, and so on. Some of roles are important, others less so. But the fundamental reality lies somewhere deep inside ourselves, and is unaltered by the choices we make – to follow one profession rather than another, to marry, to have children, to canvass for votes in local politics, or to cycle to work.

The spirit or self is the precious thing that we, uniquely, are. To live a fully satisfying and purposeful life, we need only become fully acquainted with this inner "I", to make accurate contact with ourselves, and to understand the true extent of our energy, and use it. The inner temple of the self first needs to be located (it may take some effort to clear the jungle that surrounds it), then appreciated for its potential, then renovated, then maintained. This may sound like hard work, but in fact care of the spirit is self-rewarding. We have great peace, love, power and beauty at our disposal, and the blessings we obtain by discovering these qualities within ourselves, and sending them out to the world at large, are beyond measure.

defining identity

How do I see and experience myself? This is a fundamental question, to which many of us in the modern world tend to give the wrong answers. We have fallen asleep to a true awareness of self and we define ourselves by the external rather than the internal. We are programmed to identify ourselves with things that we are not: our physical form (obsession with appearance); our job (obsession with action); our worth in relation to others (obsession with status); our material possessions (obsession with surfaces). In reality we are not these incidentals of fortune or choice, but the energy of consciousness that they clothe.

Neither are we wholly the sum of our memories, nor our relationships with others. These factors are closer to the truth, because they offer a more human dimension, a unique profile of which other people must be aware if they are to  claim that they "know" us. If we have lived responsibly and creatively, our past and our relationships will be precious to us, and they provide a picture of our lives to others. Yet these things are like a comet, making a bright, beautiful arc in the night sky. We are the fiery heart of the comet, the animating energy. We are the spirit that animates the body: identity and spirit are synonymous. Spirit is self, and its highest expressions are the radiant spiritual qualities of peace, love, truth, power and happiness.

Once truly absorbed, this realization is liberating. A great deal of personal misery is caused by the tension between the public "I" and the profound sense of an inner (frequently unfulfilled) self. If we identify ourselves too much with the public role, we become vulnerable. For example, if we lose a job or a partner we might feel that our identity is shattered. This is an illusion caused by attachment. The reality is that identity *cannot* be shattered. We have only to wake to it, and we will see that it is indivisible. In dealing with identity issues, a therapist might peel away one layer of illusion at a time, like an onion. The spiritual path, however, is transcendent, and revelation can happen in a moment. We journey within, with the help of quiet reflection to find the core of light that is our true identity.

exercise 9

the wheel of self

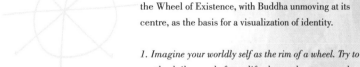

The exercise below adapts the Buddhist symbolism of the Wheel of Existence, with Buddha unmoving at its centre, as the basis for a visualization of identity.

1. Imagine your worldly self as the rim of a wheel. Try to see the daily round of your life, the people you meet, the tasks you perform, as the force that spins the wheel.

2. Now move inwards. The rim is held in place by a set of spokes. Picture each spoke as one of your personal characteristics, good or bad. One may be patience, another a tendency to see many points of view at once. Imagine as many of these spokes as you can. Notice how, when the wheel is spinning quickly, they blur and appear as a solid form. But when the wheel is turning slowly, you can examine each characteristic at leisure, and see how each contributes to your external identity.

3. Now imagine the hub of the wheel as your perfect self. You can see how the characteristics flow out from the centre, and how the rim turns about you. The nearer you get to the centre, the slower you seem to turn, until, at the absolute centre, you are perfectly still. Like your true, spiritual identity, the hub controls the wheel's speed and direction, but at its very centre it is motionless.

sovereignty of the self

The 18th-century Scottish philosopher David Hume claimed that there is no such thing as the self. What any of us calls "I" is really just a momentary constellation of perceptions, appetites, opinions and actions, given an illusion of continuity by our memories. Any successful program of spiritual growth has to reject this influential brand of pessimism. We can begin by pursuing an analogy, in which all our thoughts and feelings do in fact form bright, shifting constellations, vast and awesome when considered up close. Yet from the perspective of a spirit that fills and animates the whole universe, even the largest star-clusters dwindle to insignificance.

Spiritual growth is a process of learning how to become the rulers of our own internal universe. We can measure our progress by the mastery we have over our thoughts, feelings, needs and decisions. If we awaken to the truth that spirit is what we are, and live by that truth, we enjoy the confidence that whatever external factors put pressure on us, we remain vital and creative, and our essential spiritual nature cannot be changed.

In folktale and myth there are heroes who wear a cloak of invulnerability. Our awareness of self as spirit also makes us invincible, although not in the form of a cloak, which can be mislaid or stolen: spiritual invulnerability is at the very core of the self.

Mind (self-experience and creativity), intellect (analysis and discernment), personality (habitual behaviour patterns) and the senses (messengers to spirit) may be considered the four ministers within the self's court. To rule ourselves effectively, we take advice and evidence from each of them. A benevolent dictatorship works better than a harsh tyranny. We can even accept our limitations, so long as we do not think of them as inevitable or insurmountable. In our sovereign state, we sit at ease on our thrones, happy in possession of the kingdom within. When emotions threaten to bubble up rebelliously, we know that

Self-reverence, self-knowledge, self-control – these three alone lead to sovereign power.

•

Alfred, Lord Tennyson
(1809–1892)

we can harness and transform them through the power of intellect, chief of the four ministers.

When sensual appetites tempt us, we know that we have the strength of mind and personality to resist addiction. When criticized, we retain dignity and self-respect, rather than succumbing to defensiveness or anger. After making a mistake, we move quickly through guilt and repentance, and begin effectively and without delay to look for a solution to the problem. Emotions are recognized and acknowledged – but are allowed to pass through and beyond us, where they can do us no harm.

If we are truly in control, we realize that everyone else has the same power, and we know that we cannot control them. Nor do we have any wish to do so. Yet this type of self-sovereignty automatically translates into a form of leadership, through inspiration and influence. We shine a light that draws people to us, and inspires them to follow. We light the path of self-knowledge and thereby show others the way. And, in ruling the kingdom of self in so exemplary a fashion, our blessings spread far beyond its boundaries.

our uniqueness

A scientist once suggested that, because cooperation was such a powerful weapon in the battle for survival, early humans thrived by being "docile", or easily swayed by social pressure. It could be argued that we are a species of conformists, which is why we can be manipulated by ad-men, marketeers, war-mongers, religious zealots, and others. Certainly, we are constantly invited to compare ourselves with other people – to imitate them or to hate them, or to aspire to their wealth, beauty or power – and we may bend under the sway of such influences. Deep down, however, we have an inbuilt capacity to understand, value and preserve what is unique about every one of us – the beauty and value of the self, the treasure of our spirituality, whose discovery is the basis of self-esteem.

There are two main schools of thought about human nature. Followers of the 17th-century English thinker, Thomas Hobbes, hold that we are all essentially brutish, and have to be tamed by society. There is more opti-

> *Man makes holy what he believes, as he makes beautiful what he loves.*
>
> •
>
> Ernest Renan
> (1823–92)

mism, however, in the views of the 18th-century Romantic philosopher, Jean Jacques Rousseau, who believed that we are naturally free, virtuous and noble, and that it is society that corrupts us and forces us to conform to its unnatural and alien patterns.

Spiritual awareness may be seen as the process of connecting with and nurturing a sense of this incomparable, beautiful inner core, and working to keep ourselves from being poisoned by negative influences from others, whether individual or collective.

There is nothing egotistical about insisting on our own uniqueness. After all, being unique is the least unique thing about us: it is the one quality that we share with absolutely everyone. Furthermore, an egotist needs followers, and all we are claiming is our right not to be led.

This is an important freedom, because everybody grows at a different rate, and if we are to reach an awareness of our spirituality, we have to reach it along our own path, at our own natural pace.

beauty in a crowd

Next time you are in a crowd of people, perhaps on a bus or a train, or in the supermarket, or at a football or baseball stadium, try to think of yourself not as part of an anonymous mass, but as a flower in a vast garden.

All around are other flowers, but all belong to different species – no two are alike, as you will see if you scan the faces that surround you.

You do not feel psychic pressure in this crowd: your identity is not compromised. Ignore any negative feelings you detect among the others – impatience, for example, or grumpiness, or aggression. Instead, try to pick up the positive feelings enjoyed by others around you – the sense of freedom, exhilaration, hopefulness, and other positive energies. All crowds have something of this positive energy. You recognize everyone in the crowd as your spiritual equals. Yet, at the same time, you have a strong sense of self, and the unique beauty at the heart of self.

Think of Ezra Pound's haiku about subway commuters: "The apparition of these faces in a crowd: / Petals on a wet black bough."

responsibility

Many of us experience difficulties in reconciling the two concepts of freedom and responsibility. Yet, paradoxically, these states are not only consistent, but they depend upon each other intimately. One of the most stirring affirmations ever made about the dignity of the human spirit, the American Declaration of Independence, states that all are "endowed by their Creator with certain unalienable Rights, that these include Life, Liberty and the pursuit of Happiness". But these rights are unalienable only by virtue of our common vigilance, and our willingness to assume responsibility for maintaining them.

What is true socially is also true in the personal realm. Freedom and responsibility are like the two sides of an arch leaning in upon each other, with a truthful self-image acting as the central keystone. Unless we are free, in the sense of being able to do and say what we believe in, rather than being determined by others, responsibility means nothing but conformity.

Conversely, unless we are responsible, and live by our belief in what is right, our freedom is an indulgence – wasted, because it will bring us nothing of worth. Taking responsibility for ourselves frees us from the false dictates of society. Freedom is the only medium in which we can live virtuously.

Buddhism recognizes the idea of the *Boddhisattva*, or Buddha-to-be, the soul who postpones its passing into Buddha-hood in order to help other souls achieve salvation. This is responsibility on a grand scale. If we value ourselves, valuing others is the natural next step, and although we may stop short of full-time, self-sacrificing altruism, we will certainly want to enact good works in the world around us as much as our energy and time permit. When motivated by the energies of the spirit, duties cease to be chores and instead become ways to project our creative vision onto the world. Satisfying our physical appetites and indulging in creature comforts are pale and unfulfilling by contrast.

Responsibility does not mean being held to account for the thoughts or actions of others, but

it does involve taking upon ourselves the charge of enlightening others by actively disseminating our energy among the people with whom we come into contact. To this extent, a completely solitary life might be interpreted as incomplete. However, it is unwise to be too prescriptive, as who could deny the possibility that a solitary mystic, through his writings, might touch the souls of millions with his insights and bring about positive changes in their lives?

The mystic hermit stands at one extreme of a spectrum. Meanwhile, at the other extreme is the tireless worker for charity who does good works instinctively and unthinkingly, and spends no time on self-discovery, meditation or any other intentional spiritual exercises. We cannot say that such a person is neglecting the spirit if their virtuous energy pours out in such limitless abundance. Ten minutes of contact with them would be enough to convince us of the purity of their calling. Somehow, perhaps by some route not touched upon in this book, they have found the truth of spirit and their own way to enact it.

values

We live in a world where quantity and quality are regularly and horribly confused. Value is measured in terms of amount, and people are constantly telling us that more is better. Lists are issued comparing the relative wealth of people who are all so rich that comparisons are meaningless. Is a personal fortune of $100 billion really more satisfying than one of $50 billion? We "know" that Picasso is the greatest artist of the 20th century because his paintings fetch the highest prices. Satisfaction of all sorts is measured in terms of how often and how much. But it is impossible to give a numerical value to the facets of the spirit, such as peace, love, truth, power and happiness. More is not better. Better is better.

However, is it not the case that the more precious something becomes, the more we have to guard against its enslaving us? The truth is, it is hard for us to care *for* the things we need: instead, we tend to care *about* whether we have them or not. Need is an all-or-nothing state of mind: there is little room to manoeuvre between these two extremes in order to assign a scale of values to our experiences. If we need something, our appreciation of its qualities tends to be corrupted by a helpless attachment to it, or by the spiritually crippling fear that we are going to lose it.

Paradoxically, it is in the qualities of the spirit that need and value meet. For although we need love, purity, truth, creativity, in order to enjoy fulfilled lives, these are already ours, eternally and ineradicably. We can value these absolute spiritual necessities precisely because they are absolute, because we need never feel that we are without them, or fear that we are going to lose them. Most of us live our lives to some extent by other people's values – perhaps those of a boss, spouse or parent. The values we find for ourselves inside the spirit, however, provide a more reliable compass on life's journey.

the seven jars of value

We explore our personal values through the choices we make. How do we respond if we are challenged to prioritize between a number of different valuable commodities? We may find that some of the commodities have equal value, and we cannot decide between them.

Imagine a shelf with seven jars on it. A genie is waiting nearby for you to give him one of the jars, and you know that he may return again and again in the future, taking one jar at a time until only one is left. Picture the jars carefully. The first is plain clay, caked with mud, but you can see some archaic patterns where the surface is exposed: this contains ancient wisdom about the workings of the spirit. The second is shaped like a beautiful soaring bird, and contains positive thoughts. The third is still gift-wrapped, and contains the good wishes we have for our friends. The fourth is like a perfume bottle, and contains a magical balm, which will soothe away all our worries. The fifth is a spherical container, balanced on the shoulders of a porcelain figure, and contains emotional support from your closest friend. The sixth is clear glass, with handfuls of diamonds within – these are the creative talents. The seventh is shaped like a pair of cupped hands, and contains blessings from your parents. Choose which jar to give away immediately, and then decide in what order you will give them up in future, should you ever have to do so.

ego and humility

If we believe in the sovereignty of the self, are we not in danger of falling prey to egotism and arrogance? If fulfilment of one's spiritual potential involves journeying into oneself, how can we justify this in relation to our care for humanity as a whole? These questions bring us to one of the most challenging paradoxes of the spirit – the way in which our inward journey spreads its blessings outward into the world at large. By cultivating the individual soul and harvesting its truths, we become more inclined and better equipped to give – to radiate love to those all around us.

People of a sceptical cast of mind might interpret the inner quest as an act of ego, or a symptom of an inflated ego, but to think in this way is to misunderstand. Ego is the most serious disease of spirit, and certainly a terminal condition of spiritual awareness. Deep spiritual healing is no more nor less than the eradication of ego. And when we consent to undergo the healing process, it is as if our egotism and our spirituality

In the intellectual order, the virtue of humility is nothing more nor less than the power of attention.

.

Simone Weil
(1909–43)

contend for mastery within the arena of the self. Self-understanding, self-possession and self-worth are on the side of the spirit; selfishness, pride and insecurity are on the side of the ego.

But what about self-importance? This is actually one of those terms whose meaning in common speech is at odds with its literal meaning. If I feel that my life, or my comfort, or my convenience, is more important than that of someone else, then I am profoundly and spiritually misguided. On the other hand, if I feel that my spiritual health is not important, then I am committing an equally grave error.

Our spiritual health is in fact the key to living happily and helpfully as a human being, for how can we love others if we do not have profound respect for ourselves as a starting-point? Hence the crucial importance of the journey within: it is not an ostrich-like withdrawal from the priorities of life, but an essential act of orientation, to arrive at a true perspective on ourselves in the context of everything that is not ourselves (other

people, material phenomena, time, and everything that makes up our surroundings).

In certain mystical traditions there is a strand of self-hatred – the belief that an individual human soul is worthless when seen in the light of the divine. Nothing could be further from the understanding that lies at the heart of this book. Each individual human soul has an eternal connection with the source of spirit. Although we may have lost awareness of this personal relationship with the divine, we are all the bearers of its highest spiritual qualities. Our original nature has qualities reflective of divinity, which we see in the voice of conscience and the spontaneity of love.

To clarify this further, we can think of the battle between spirit and ego as a battle between the broad-sighted and the narrow-sighted. If ego gains a foothold, I see my life in the narrowest perspective, in terms of short-term gains. I will treat other people as a means to my own selfish ends. If, on the other hand, I become spiritually aware, I see my own life in the widest perspective. Other people acquire tremendous importance in this broad understanding of things. My purpose is to rain my spiritual gifts upon others, to radiate love in all directions. Not least of the paradoxes of the spirit is that a proper respect for the sacredness of the self leads to selflessness.

truth and honesty

Truthfulness is honesty – fidelity to the facts. But truth is something different – less literal and more profound. The important thing is truth to ourselves – fidelity to our inner voice, the voice of profound wisdom (not always the same as popular wisdom), conscience (not to be confused with peer pressure or inherited dogma), and instinctive self-understanding (not the same as instinct *per se*).

Truth is best seen as a benchmark of the spiritually-aware life. *Are we being true?* we might ask ourselves. Are we true to ourselves and others? If the answer is no, something is amiss. It is as if at our spiritual core we have a bedrock of solid truths that tell us what is right and what is wrong. So that, usually, we will know the answer deep down, without having to think too hard. Truth finds its way to the surface. That is not to say, however, that we will not unconsciously put obstacles in its way. Full self-knowledge means that we understand these obstacles. Living by that self-knowledge – living in spiritual awareness – means that we remove these obstacles.

Perhaps, for various reasons, some of us will find the question of whether or not we are being true more difficult to answer. We might think that we are being true (truthful is not quite the same thing), but we may be uncertain. If so, we know that we need to work at something in our lives. If we are in a fully aware state, we will answer *yes* with complete confidence.

How does truth relate to veracity – that is, giving a literally factual answer to a question, or making a statement that could be verified by checking the facts? This is a fundamental moral issue, which can be boiled down to a simple question: is it acceptable to tell a lie? We all know how bad it feels to lie – our discomfort shows us that we were aware of the truth, even though we chose not to use it. We feel guilty when we are serving our own interests by lying, or being cowardly. In fact, these feelings are a sign that we know the

I speak the truth, not so much as I would wish, but as much as I dare; and I dare a little more, as I grow older.

·

Michel de Montaigne
(1533–92)

difference between what is right and what is wrong. We might lie for the sake of someone else, to avoid hurting their feelings or to prevent them from facing up to an unpleasant or painful situation. However, our motivation, though seemingly altruistic, may in fact be self-interest in disguise. When we withhold information (for example, failing to tell a friend that we disapprove of an aspect of their behaviour), are we really being selfless, or are we censoring the truth for the sake of our own peace of mind? Issues absorb energy, as we know deep in our hearts: when we jealously guard our secrets, we

may be opting, unconsciously, to preserve our energy. The key to understanding ourselves is to be watchful of such tricks of the ego.

Truth can be a powerful agent for change, and when we release it into the world we must do so with accuracy and care. What we say to others is one of the gifts that derive from spirit, even if our message at times is necessarily unpalatable. Not to be aware of the impact of our words would be an arrogance, a failure of empathy. To give truth excessive emphasis or to let it out too quickly can sometimes be just as regrettable as neglecting to tell the truth at all.

letting go

Sometimes the most difficult things to do are those that language makes us feel should be easy: focusing on our own thoughts, forgiving ourselves for our mistakes, making time for contemplation. One of these deceptively easy-sounding actions is letting go. We often spend much of our time concentrating our energies in order to gain something: more possessions, more territory, more understanding. But, in fact, the various important projects we may have in our lives are not damaged by periods of deliberately doing, and thinking about, something else. We remain the same person if we spend a week on a retreat without giving a single thought to even some of our cherished friendships. Such periods of letting go are refreshing and balancing. More profoundly, letting go means moderating excessive attachment to material possessions, to emotions, or to the status quo in our lives. In a world where objects are designed to be cherished, we can refuse to have our values corrupted by the false allure of covetable things. Current teaching is to give our emotions free rein, because repression brings inner turbulence. However, letting them run wild simply causes outward discord and chaos in the world. A more valuable option is to let emotions go and thus attain peace. And if the status quo is a comfort zone, here too it is valuable to identify what ties we should sever, in order to be freed from unreliable dependencies.

putting things in their place

The term *fetish* comes from a Portuguese word meaning "charm". It was used by 16th-century sailors to describe what they thought of as bizarre objects, made of wood and rag, and worshipped by the natives of western Africa. Although the sailors considered the fetishes to be worthless, they were held in great esteem by the Africans, who believed that they were the homes of spirits. In the modern West, we are surrounded by our own versions of the fetish – cars, houses, clothing, electronic gadgets, and so on. Tragically, the spirit with which we invest these objects is our own. Many of us allow them to define our worth, and we make their acquisition one of the central goals of our lives.

To those of us trying to escape this trap, materialism appears as the arch-enemy of spirituality. The sage must not be wedded to the world, we claim, and usually cite ascetic figures, such as Gandhi, to support this opinion. At the same time, wealth seems to preclude compassion, patience and wisdom. Materialism and pride in wealth are linked with ego, and its characteristic activity of acquisition as a means to define (erroneously) self-worth.

However, anti-materialism can become just as much of a fetish, and just as inimical to the growth of the soul. One Native American tribe used to hold festivals called potlatches, where people gave away or destroyed their own possessions. Valuable commodities such as canoes and sea-otter pelts were ceremonially burned. In time the spiritual dimension evaporated from the festival, as the tribe become more and more concerned about social status. The potlatches became competitive. Failing to match a rival's display of generosity meant a humiliating loss of face.

There is a lesson in the potlatch. Shunning the material world is not an automatic source of spiritual benefit. What we need to turn away from is the attitude that our belongings reflect our intrinsic worth. There is nothing harmful in shopping for something beautiful that gives us pleasure. The danger arises when what we shop for gives us pride, affirmation or reassurance. So-called "retail therapy" might make us feel better in the short term, but it reinforces an impoverished sense of self as little more than a pattern of ownership. When we devote our energies

to money or material possessions, we distract ourselves from our purpose in life. The more we feed our material appetite, the hungrier it becomes.

At their best, material possessions provide a link with the past, and a message to the future. Even native peoples who transmit their culture orally will pass on heirlooms as a kind of seal of authenticity on the stories they tell.

If we were to place no value on what was outside ourselves, in the material world, there would be no art, no technology and probably no change. The challenge is to remind ourselves that our own worth is innate and inviolable, and that the worth of any object – whether it be a painting or a sportscar – lies in what it is, its beauty or usefulness and not in whether we can aspire to own it one day, or fear its loss.

By surrounding ourselves with possessions, we create distractions and defences, causing ourselves to feel enslaved. But in our enlightened self-awareness, we put things in their rightful place, and thereby regain our freedom. With this comes a whole new way of looking at the world, and being in the world.

putting emotions in their place

Curiously, Western culture, whose attitudes have been so much influenced by the economic and political status of the male, shares with many mystical disciplines a mistrust of emotions. Because reason is what separates us from the animals, the argument runs, it is upon giving due emphasis to reason that our hopes of fulfilment depend – whether in the social or the personal sphere. However, modern psychology contends that, rather than mastering our emotions, we should live in equilibrium with them, and use the energy that they give us – an energy associated by many with the strength of the feminine. By repressing our emotions, it is said, we put ourselves on the road to psychic imbalance, and are denied happiness.

The question, *What should we do about emotions?* is central to finding spiritual awareness. First, we need to understand what emotions are. This can be difficult, as we tend to be too close to them to perceive them clearly. Standing back at a distance, and viewing our emotions objectively, is a valuable part of learning to deal with them. Emotions are hard to come to terms with because we experience them as chemical surges that seem unwilling to negotiate with both the more reasonable parts of ourselves and with the loving parts. The chemistry of emotions is not fully understood, but we can still grasp their nature as the tumult of the ego while it strains unsuccessfully to shape the world to its own will.

At the end of the 19th century, the psychologist William James made a radical attack on the commonsense idea that when we see a bear, for example, we automatically become frightened and run away. James suggested that in fact we see the bear, instinctively run away, and then feel fear because we are running. The emotion is caused by the physiological response to some

*Often where the wind
has gathered
The trees together,*

*One tree will take
Another in her arms
and hold.*

*Their branches that
are grinding
Madly together and
together,*

*It is no real fire.
They are breaking
each other.*

.

Paul Muldoon
(b.1952)

stimulus, not the other way round. Although this idea has not proved persuasive in its original form, one of its offshoots is the "attitudinal theory", which says that our postures and expressions are vital factors in shaping the emotions we feel. Thus, for example, smiling, genuinely and warmly, is a good antidote to anger, as is sitting calmly and practising breath control. We can achieve balance in our minds by adjusting the posture or attitude of our bodies.

In time, we can all learn to transform emotions into neutral or positive feelings consistent with spiritual peace. When you feel the first stirrings of the storm rolling through you, treat this as the signal to still yourself and observe what is happening. Imagine that you are a bystander on the riverbank watching the flood surge by. By keeping mentally as still as possible, slowing down your thinking, living in the moment, and concentrating at the same time on breathing deeply, you will find that the flood begins to subside.

It may help to think of the emotion as a tide or backwash that is disturbing your true flow of life, the movement of spirit. We live in a mental space where these tides happen, frequently and unpredictably. But if we learn the art of allowing them to flow through us without affecting how we think and behave, we will find that our spiritual current runs its true, peaceful course.

Dealing with emotions, we might imagine, is an art that cannot be rehearsed: every time we cope with anger, or jealousy, or lust, it is for real, in response to some stimulus that we are unable to control. This is not quite the case, however, because we also feel strong emotions in recollection. For example, when describing to a friend our fury over a work colleague's unreasonable behaviour, we often relive the tempest. To practise emotional acceptance, try reliving an upsetting incident in your memory, as vividly as possible, until you can do so calmly. Repeat the circumstances aloud to yourself, quoting any dialogue in the original incident. You might consider making a sound recording of your story, working away at it until all tremulous traces of emotion are ironed out. Once you have mastered this, try telling the tale to a friend without becoming emotionally involved. Imagine the scene as if you were an impartial onlooker. Or imagine that you are in court and that every sign of emotion will annoy the judge, adding years to your sentence. Such exercises may soon have a purifying effect, distancing you from emotional surges.

In real-life situations too, it can help to change the perspective. This can be done spatially, as described above, so that you appear to be experiencing the emotional situation through another's eyes. You might even raise your viewpoint mentally into the air until you and whoever else is involved become tiny figures in a landscape, seen from above. Or, try to enlarge the dimension of time rather than space. Step back in your imagination and think of the incident you are experiencing as a moment in the past, recollected from the future. How will you feel about it in a year's time? Imagine yourself as an older, wiser person, who has time-travelled to visit a period of emotional turbulence – like a tourist observing antiquated customs in some time-locked country. Such mental devices create new patterns in your inner world, and eventually you will no longer need them, as emotional distancing becomes a reflex of the spirit.

exercise 10

the witness and the whirlwind

Sometimes in a state of high emotion we can feel as if we are caught up in a whirlwind. We need to find ways to achieve a sense of detachment, to locate the storm's calm centre, so that we can regain our bearings.

1. Recollect some emotionally turbulent episode from your past. Choose one that you found confusing, with many conflicting emotions.

2. Imagine yourself sitting in a swivel-chair on a slightly raised podium, being interrogated by a number of people, each of whom represents one of your emotions. Each one takes a turn at asking you to describe the event or events in question.

3. At first you may feel like swivelling in the chair to face your questioner. Gradually resist the impulse. Sit facing forward and make each questioner walk in front of you. Slowly imagine them circling you more quickly.

4. Watch how they become a soothing blur in front of your eyes, as their voices merge into a relaxing hum. Try to think of all your emotions, especially those that accuse or entreat, whirling around you, leaving you impassive and relaxed at the centre.

finding non-attachment

Attachment is the condition from which we suffer when we are incapable of acceptance. In our lack of belief in ourselves, we cling to material possessions as substitutes for self-worth; we become fixed in our habits, especially those that give us pleasure; we react emotionally when life does not go as planned, or when the ego sees opportunities for inflating itself. Attachments encumber the spirit: what the ego designs as anchors become shackles, although we are not aware of them as such.

Suppose that you invite me to give you some spiritual advice, and I recommend that you give up your regular Saturday shopping treats. You might feel that you are a loser in this transaction, whereas you are not losing but shedding. *My Saturdays mean so much to me*, you plead. In fact, the value you set on them needs to be inverted. The amount that you think you have lost is the amount that actually you have gained, many times over. In taking my advice you make a clearing in the thicket of attachment, in which you may recover the gift of the self.

Emotional attachment is trickier territory, in part because emotions are often wrongly held to be valid in themselves. But peace comes from letting our emotions flow right through us, out into the distance, where they can do no harm.

Non-attachment does not mean letting go of responsibility, commitment or love: it means seeing those things unemotionally, in the context of the higher values – responsibility and commitment that are chosen, not enforced by social pressure; love that is selfless, not food for the ego.

Imagine that your partner one day announces that he or she feels a deep-seated need to leave. The pain you feel in letting this person be themselves is the pain of attachment; the courage you show in giving your blessing to the break-up is an upwelling of love from the spirit. Non-attachment is the way to peace, because it places value beyond the realm in which we are vulnerable – that is, in the world of spirit, which is changeless, not in the world of emotional dependency, which changes beyond our control.

exercise 11

the garden of the world

At the heart of non-attachment is the knowledge that life is a state of flux. Emotional states and the relationships they nurture are always changing. Some will die, but something will always grow in their place.

1. Picture your mind as a garden that needs tending. If you are already feeling trapped by commitments, begin by imagining the garden choked with weeds, perhaps containing a disused fountain and a stagnant pond.

2. Every day, go into the garden and do a little more work. Cut back the weeds, and with every one you remove, allow yourself a new freedom – a small respite from the demands that clutter up your life.

3. Unblock the fountain. See the flowing water as your personal spiritual fountain cascading the positive qualities and virtues of spirit (for example, peace, love, truth, power, happiness). If you get discouraged, drink from it, or let it pour over you and feel it refreshing you.

4. Imagine healthy relationships as blooming flowers. See if you can find things that could be pruned (habits and routines). You are giving vitality back to the plant, and making room for a new bloom, a deeper aspect of the relationship, to grow.

the way of least resistance

A central idea of many faiths is that it is not only useless, but counterproductive, to resist a threatening force. Resistance will only make it stronger. Yielding to a situation is often the best way to survive it – a point often emphasized in the parable of the reed that bends before the wind, while the oak tree is snapped in two. There is no such thing as an immovable object. Faced by the awesome power of nature, by the obstacles that may lie in the path of our hopes and dreams, inflexibility is the catalyst of our own self-destruction.

This approach to life is explored most fully in Daoism, a philosophy that arose in China more than 2,000 years ago. Although the central expression of Daoist thought is found in the *Dao De Jing*, traditionally written by the sage Lao Zi, it is likely that the first Daoists were hermits, mentioned in early Chinese chronicles as "those who obscure themselves". Their ideas stress the difficulty of living in a society driven by power struggles and personal ambition. According to the *Dao De Jing*, even a king should avoid such temptations, and should "act only by inactivity", believing that the state would thrive as a matter of course, in the natural order of things, and according to what should be.

The "non-action" (*wu-wei*) of the Daoists is not weakness or laziness, but involves doing only what is perfectly natural and spontaneous, so that whatever happens seems to happen of its own accord. The sage achieves this by merging perfectly with the *Dao* (Way) – the eternal, creative force that is the beginning and end of all things – so that it flows through him without obstacle. In this way he too becomes boundless and immortal. He also acts, like the *Dao*, without assertiveness or partiality. In common with most other mystical traditions, Daoism recommends meditation to empty the

> *Dao is the eternal without doing and yet nothing remains undone.*
>
> ...
>
> *What is half shall become whole. What is crooked shall become straight. What is empty shall become full.*
>
> ...
>
> *Without going outdoors one knows the world. Without looking out of the window one sees the Dao of Heaven. The further out one goes, the lesser one's knowledge becomes.*
>
> ·
>
> Dao De Jing
> (6th or 5th century BC)

mind and allow a union with the Dao that goes deeper than conscious thought; and breath control to facilitate the flow of universal energy through the body.

Desire is the chief distraction from the true path, and is usually compounded by a worldly education, which tends to make us want more. Enlightenment is a process of unlearning, and returning to a state of simplicity. Many Daoist parables preach the value of being "useless", like a tree with knotted wood.

There is a phrase that neatly sums up the classic human response to a threatening situation: "fight or flight". It is easy to feel, particularly in the competitive modern world, that if we do not contend with a situation, then we are, shamefully, running away from it. Fleeing, of course, suggests fear – another emotion. Why is there not a third option? Why do we not stand still and face up to a situation – taking in its meaning, and then absolving ourselves of its impact?

Daoism, and the schools of philosophy and martial arts arising from it, teach this third way. According to ancient legend, the fighting and exercise system known as *T'ai Chi Chuan* was invented by a 12th-century recluse called Chang San Feng, after he watched a battle between a crane and a snake. During the contest, the writhing movements of the snake made the stabbing of the crane's beak completely ineffective. The hermit saw this as proof of the dictum in verse 43 of the *Dao De Jing*: "The most yielding of things in the universe overcomes the most hard."

The *T'ai Chi Chuan Classics*, compiled in the 19th century, eloquently sum up the principles of the system: "One should yield at the slightest pressure, and adhere at the slightest retreat. The entire body is so sensitive that not a feather may be added without setting it in motion. The spirit is calm and the body peaceful. Be aware of the direction of the mind."

Sensitivity is more important than strength, and success comes not from mastering a set of circumstances, but from responding to them with the greatest degree of freedom, immediacy and spontaneity.

There is an interesting parallel to be found in the emotional health of families. Behavioural therapists have found that the families with greatest problems are those in which parents and children are either completely intransigent, or absolutely terrified of conflict, and willing to do anything to avoid it. The healthiest families live

as if they are playing a game, constantly testing the strength and nature of their relationships, but always reacting quickly and sympathetically to each others' moods. The way of least resistance in worldly and social terms means just that – acknowledging, hearing and taking on board issues and problems, but then giving ourselves the permission and the freedom to disperse them. Emotions cannot cloud spirit when they have been set free.

There is a *T'ai Chi Chuan* exercise that provides a flavour of this type of free-floating sensitivity, and can also be used as a meditative aid. Sit facing a partner, quite close together. Both of you should hold out your hands, palms facing forward, and place your palms flat against your partner's. You should both begin to push back and forth, but after a time one of you (decide which before you start) should try to concentrate on following their partner's movements (stop resisting them), and try not to initiate any of their own. In time, with luck, you will be astonished to see your hands swimming back and forth, apparently of their own accord. Once you have mastered the technique, as you do it close your eyes and focus on the flow of your hands.

exercise 12

flowing uphill

This exercise was once described by a monk, while making the pre-dawn climb up Adam's Peak in Sri Lanka. It shows how effortless the most arduous tasks can be, if they are approached in the right way. The challenge is to climb a hill, a mountain or the stairs in a high-rise building – a climb that would normally be tiring, that you may not normally attempt.

1. Climb as slowly as you can imagine possible, and then slow down even more. You are like a chameleon slowly stalking its prey along a branch. As you climb, concentrate on breath entering and leaving your body.

2. When you are relaxed, imagine a hand at your back, gently pushing you upward. Start to think of yourself as flowing up the hill or staircase. Experience this as a physical sensation and visualize the movement, its natural speed and grace. If you lose this sense of flowing, are distracted, or begin moving too fast, go back to the first step and concentrate on your breathing.

3. It is easy to tell if you have done the exercise properly. You will reach the top of the stairs, hill or mountain more relaxed and full of energy than when you started.

the gifts of the world

If spirit is pure and without form, and enfolds beauty within itself, how are we to regard the multiplicity of the world around us? How are we to relate to the endlessly absorbing phenomena that we experience through our senses? If we ascribe beauty to nature or the arts, while at the same time insisting that all ultimate values lie within, are we being contradictory? In fact, there is no conflict of meaning, because whatever we experience as beauty is a gift – a reassurance that our outpouring of love upon the world is returned to us in a perfect exchange. As we experience a superb vista, a graceful portrait, or a heart-melting string quartet, our spirit looks in a mirror and sees its own beauty reflected there in sensory form. Our senses are messengers that bring us up-to-date bulletins of our circumstances. One of our birthrights is nature, which brims over with objects on which the spirit may rest its gaze. At the same time the natural world offers a quiet setting for meditation, with a wealth of symbols that can point the way to spiritual insight. Another birthright is imagination, whose power is shown in works that offer us tantalizing, inspiring glimpses of eternal truths. Yet, we are all artists, whose masterwork is the enlightened self and the uses to which self-awareness is put. An act of love or forgiveness is a creative act that illuminates the world.

landscape and the senses

A belief in the value and beauty of nature, on the one hand, and in the reality of our spiritual beauty, on the other, are mutually reinforcing. Spiritual awareness is the opposite of egotism: it is a profound self-respect that brims over and flows ceaselessly into a radiating selfless love. This outwelling of love pours into other people, potentially enriching their spirit also. Yet the love we give if we are spiritually aware is not exclusive – we do not select individuals for special treatment – but a boundless flow in all directions. So the flow of our love pours out over the natural world too, informing it with meaning and purpose. At the same time, we are grateful, as we must be for all good things. This gratitude, a sense of love reciprocated, is at the heart of our experience of beauty.

Modern ways of life have put a distance between ourselves and nature. This is a pity, because when we look out over mountains or valleys, a lake or a forest, watch the sun rise or sink, or observe in close-up the intricate rib-pattern of a leaf, we experience a material reflection of our own spiritual beauty. It

*The soil, in return
for her service,
keeps the tree tied
to her; the sky
asks nothing
and leaves it free.*

•

Rabindranath Tagore
(1861–1941)

is only via the beauty of the spirit, our own inward beauty, that we admire nature. We have been born with special privileges, and it would be wasteful not to use them. The outward beauty of nature is not the greatest value, being outshone by the beauty of the spirit. Yet it is a pledge of our special faculties as human beings, and answers to our spiritual powers if not to our spiritual needs. A marvellous flower, or a fine view of the Grand Canyon, is a reminder of the spirit in the same way that the call of wild swans is a reminder of the swans themselves.

Sometimes, loosely, we might speak of nature as "sublime", but this is in fact potentially misleading. The word was used by the Romantics in the late 18th and early 19th centuries to express the feelings of awe inspired by a vertiginous peak, waterfall or chasm. There was a frisson of self-abasement in this – the idea of the microscopic human being standing powerless in the palm of God's hand. However, rather than thrilling masochistically to the sublime, a more accurate response would be to recognize the self's

sovereignty. With nature at our feet and our finger-
tips, we are truly commanders of all we survey. What
better place than a hilltop, or a mountain summit if
we have the energy, far from human distractions, to
be quiet and still in meditation?

The answer to this question might be, a garden.
Gardens are the opposite of the sublime – nature
tamed by human creativity rather than present
in all its awe-inspiring force – and as places for
contemplation, whether seated or walking, have
the advantage of being less strenuous to reach.
Wandering randomly through a garden, deciding
which path to follow only at the very last moment,

taking time to appreciate the flowers or berries, the
shades of green, the changing surface underfoot,
the sudden views that open up, and the artistry of
the design – these experiences add up to a refined
sensory pleasure, and at the same time provide a
relaxed opportunity for the gentle meditative play
of our spirit over the world's surfaces.

The landscape, whether natural or "improved" by
farmers or gardeners, is rich in outward images that
reflect profound inner realities. Often in literature
from the Middle Ages onwards we come across
references to nature as a book of wisdom: we have
only to turn its pages (in other words, walk within

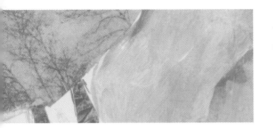

the landscape or garden) to find inspiring moral lessons. The tree is emblematic of patience and strength, the reed of pliancy, the flower of beauty or virtue; also, individual flowers, especially in Victorian times, had their own symbolism. This idea can be adapted for the purposes of self-discovery: for "moral" we can equally well read "spiritual". Try this next time you go on a walk in a landscape. For example, you might feel that a rocky path represents the challenges that you need to overcome on your spiritual journey: itemize them as you follow the route. At the end of the path a little stream might tinkle into a pool – perhaps the music of spiritual fulfilment. Or there might be a shady clump of ivy – their sinuous tendrils representing the far-reaching influence of spiritual energy.

Such exercises are instructive as ways to open up the mind to new ways of thinking. They stretch the imagination, and make it more supple. However, they are best done on an occasional rather than a regular basis, because they carry with them the danger of over-intellectualizing the world of sensual

experiences. This brings us to a paradox at the heart of many forms of meditation. On the one hand, the ideal is to be self-aware, to be conscious of ourselves as pure spirit; yet at the same time we aim to be mindful, to experience phenomena directly through the senses without the interference pattern of the ego distorting our perceptions. To be in nature, away from social distractions, is the perfect circumstance for achieving this delicate balance. Aware of the spirit as the ultimate good and the ultimate reality, we perceive the raindrop roll down the leaf and fall to the earth – a moment of time purely apprehended within the spirit's all-encompassing command.

Find a little patch of nature near to your home and get to know it intimately – perhaps a little corner of a wood, or the edge of a pond, or a tucked-away grove in a public park. Visit at all times of year, and observe the changes that the seasons bring about, as well as the growth from one year to the next. Tend the spot – for example, by clearing away any litter, or making sure that any flowers are not driven out by more invasive vegetation. Think of yourself when visiting this place as making a little spiritual pilgrimage, and be sure to practise some meditation. Bring leaves or other souvenirs back for your own home as tokens of the beauty that lies in wait beyond the drone of the city.

exercise 13

a country walk

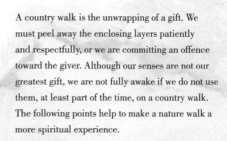

A country walk is the unwrapping of a gift. We must peel away the enclosing layers patiently and respectfully, or we are committing an offence toward the giver. Although our senses are not our greatest gift, we are not fully awake if we do not use them, at least part of the time, on a country walk. The following points help to make a nature walk a more spiritual experience.

1. Appreciate the sounds and smells. These are as much nature's gifts as the sights. Think of the sounds as the music of nature, the smells as its breath. If a wind is blowing, you are doubly blessed: watch how it moves among the trees, bushes and grasses; see how it lifts birds in flight.

2. Vary your focus, from close to distant views. Get into the habit of crouching down for close observation of tiny flowers, insects and so on. Look at the clouds, and the changing light on scenes that are far, far away.

3. Closely observe the flowers, trees or birds that you see. If you know them already, try to reach beyond their names and the characteristics by which you recognize them, and perceive them as if for the very first time.

finding richness in the moment

Imagine that you are cooking a meal for friends, following a recipe in a book. You have all the ingredients you need – vegetables, herbs, nuts, spices – and you have an hour and a half to do the cooking before your first guests arrive. You follow the instructions to the letter, and as you do so your thoughts drift to the people you have invited round to your home. Will everyone get on together, will so-and-so still be preoccupied with the crisis in her professional life, is such-and-such still thinking of moving to the mountains? – and so on. After 50 minutes or

so you have finished the cooking and laid the table. But freeze the moment there! Look back on the physical experience of the cooking, as distinct from the mental speculation. Do you remember the smells released, the textures and colours of the raw ingredients, the sound of the knife on the chopping board? Preparing a meal can be a rich and complex sensory experience. But unless you were "mindful" – that is, unless you savoured the moments as you experienced them – this experience would have eluded you. And the answer to all these questions might be: *No, I don't remember.*

Mindfulness is the art of seeing that every moment has a value of its own, even if the experience of that moment does not connect with any of our ambitions, or goals, or mental preoccupations. To spotlessly clean a window, or sweep leaves from the backyard, is a physical experience that has its own significance and nobility. This is one reason why monks in many faiths recognize the spiritual value of routine agricultural work, such as digging, planting and other activities that we might normally consider tedious or banal.

exercise 14

a *"mindful"* adventure

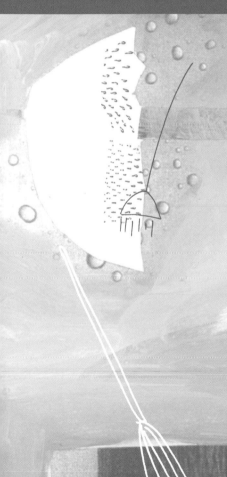

This exercise can be centred around any routine house-hold chore. We will take the sweeping of leaves as an example, but we could equally well choose any of the other repetitive tasks that tend to inspire us with boredom or even dread – from peeling potatoes, to clearing the attic, to painting a fence. You can do the exercise in reality or, if no such chore requires doing, as a highly realized visualization (in which case, sit comfortably in a quiet place, close your eyes and vividly conjure up the images in your mind).

preparation

As you contemplate the task ahead, vow to yourself that you will concentrate on the physical experience in itself, and not get distracted by thoughts of what you will do after you have finished, or by the clock ticking away, or by a sense of frustration at the slowness of the work.

execution

As you perform your task of sweeping, be alert with all your senses. Hear the sound of the broom swishing, the crackle of the bag into which you decant the leaves. Smell the subtle aromas released by the leaves as you disturb them. Look at the leaves' shapes and colours – all the fabled sensual richness of autumn lies herein.

moon and stars

We have become habituated to the limitations of our senses, which reach no further than the limits imposed by our biology. After all, we can only eat what is within arms' reach, reproduce with someone we can touch, protect a child whose cries we can hear. Touch and taste are confined to the body's dimensions. Smell is short-range. Hearing is medium-range (if we can hear the waterfall ahead as we drift downstream on our raft, we have a better chance of survival). The fifth sense – sight – can reach a horizon 10–15 miles off, maybe even further.

However, gazing at the night sky, we can also discern stars that are hundreds of light-years away. It is perhaps our amazing ability to see that offers the most thought-provoking speculation about spirit.

The Pleiades or Seven Sisters, a star cluster 415 light-years away, is not difficult to observe on a clear night in winter in the northern hemisphere. When we take the trouble to do this, or to pick out any other cluster or constellation, we are making a humble gesture toward the infinite, acknowledging its existence by reaching out as far as we can with the faculties at our disposal.

Contemplating the night sky, once regarded as the dwelling of the gods, brings us closer to the spiritual. If we ask ourselves why we find the night sky beautiful, we do not automatically think of reasons that fall within the same category as terrestrial forms of beauty. The night sky (excluding the moon for the moment) is a vastness randomly scattered with points of light. If we feel that terms like "purity", "immensity" and "absolute" have something to do with our response, could it not be that the joy we take in the stars wells up from the same source inside ourselves that responds, or has the potential to respond, so joyfully to the spirit? "As above, so below," runs a phrase used by astrologers to summarize the mystical connections between the heavens and our earthly destinies, the macrocosm and the microcosm. We might, with some justice, apply the same motto to the parallel between the cosmos represented for us by the night sky and the infinities of spirit within us – perhaps at the most profound level there is no distinction between the two?

Meditate on the moon. Look at it through binoculars, ideally when it is three-quarters full, because that is when its craters will be most

distinct. For as long as you can, hold the moon's features in your gaze. Observe the sharply etched crater walls, and the dark patches, the "seas". Lay down the binoculars, close your eyes and retain the image you have seen in your mind as you dwell on these thoughts.

There is no poetry, nor anything else expressed by language, that is more profound than the image you have just let into your mind. Nor is there anything more beautiful or more true: imagine this beauty and truth spilling in infinite abundance as a gift of light from the spiritual source reflecting on your own spirit, in the same way that the sun reflects off the moon. Or, alternatively, think of a great sage, long dead, whose enlightened wisdom is still reflected out into the world by our souls many generations later.

The moon is beyond change. We would never dream of wanting to alter or influence it, nor have we the slightest regret that the same face of the moon is turned always toward us: we have no need to see the dark side. Extend this deep feeling of acceptance to the whole solar system and its laws, including the Earth and its seasons, its cycle of life and death, and the indestructibility of spirit.

wonders of nature's workings

The idea of a lost paradise, a marvellous time when nature was benign and the lion lay down with the lamb, has a firm grip on the human imagination. Many myths around the world ascribe the ruthlessness of the animal kingdom, in defending territory and capturing prey, to the misdeeds of humanity, which brought violence to a world that had previously been peaceful and perfect. This golden age haunts our dreams. "Eden" is a word that positively glows with nostalgia.

The idea of natural perfection also tends to colour our everyday thinking, to the extent that many of us have an idealized view of the natural world. Others, more scientific in their outlook, find nature fascinating for its boundless ingenuity, and to such people the mechanisms of reproduction, locomotion and predation in different species are a source of wonder and an object of enthusiastic study and fieldwork.

The scientific view, of course, requires a suspension of the moral faculties, in recognition of the fact that morality is the exclusive preserve of humans. Certainly, this attitude is preferable to the widespread tendency to see the animal kingdom as a collection of clever or lovable eccentrics, put on Earth to entertain humankind.

Sentimentalism over animals can give us a distorted view of nature and of our own special status as human beings, guardians of the spiritual estate. However, that is not to say that animals do not share in the spirit. Hunters of the Far North give thanks to the spirit of the animal they are about to kill: if they omit this ceremonial preamble, it is believed that the spirit of the dead creature will not return within a new body for further hunting. Many vegetarians (myself included) have a spiritual basis for their restricted diet; others believe in the rights of animals as individuals, which is an incomplete version of the same idea (individuality and spirit are one and the same).

Despite the philosophical and ethical problems posed by the animal kingdom, we have only to

> *The wild gander leads*
> *his flock through the*
> *cool night,*
> *Ya-honk! he says, and*
> *sounds it down to me*
> *like an invitation;*
> *The pert may suppose*
> *it meaningless, but I*
> *listen closer,*
> *I find its purpose and*
> *place up there toward*
> *the November sky.*
>
> ·
>
> *Walt Whitman*
> *(1819–92)*

spend five minutes watching a hummingbird sipping from a flower, or a dragonfly darting over a ditch, to be reminded of nature's beauty, which resonates with the beauty of the spirit. To get to know nature intimately, as Henry Thoreau did from his cabin by Walden Pond in Massachusetts in the mid-19th century, is for many an act of homage. Thoreau felt himself to be a privileged witness. He wrote: "I once had a sparrow alight on my shoulder for a moment while I was hoeing in a village garden, and I felt that I was more distinguished by that circumstance than I should have been by any epaulette I could have worn."

Those who take an observant, reflective approach to the countryside and its creatures are nearer to spirit than those who use nature purely as an outdoor gymnasium for climbing, mountain-biking and skiing, a source of adrenaline highs. See nature up close: the beauty in the details is astounding, and offers fitting subject matter for the spirit's perceptions. By removing us from the frantic world of time management and emotional stress, and putting us among lives over which we have (or should have) no control, the shy bustlings of wildlife amid the patient world of trees and plants, nature reinforces in us the habit of acceptance.

the visual imagination

Plato was suspicious of art. God created the idea of the (noumenal) bed, the carpenter made real (phenomenal) beds, the painter copied the mere appearance of a bed, without understanding how it was made. Art that aspires to the spiritual is even more dangerous, because it is soothing, it persuades us that we are already wise and virtuous and that we need make no further effort. The artist makes the work for us: we remain passive but nevertheless claim our share in the work's greatness. Intuitively, we reject Plato's criticism while accepting that the inward glimpses provided by great art are no substitute for living a life of love based on self-understanding and the spiritual beauty of giving. Perhaps great art can be an inspiration on this journey – not rocket fuel, but a porthole that provides energizing views. Certainly, when we look into a painting we forget the materials and workmanship and we confront a scene of the imagination made miraculously visible. If the painting is a great

> *What art offers is space – a certain breathing room for the spirit.*
>
> ·
>
> *John Updike*
> *(b. 1932)*

one, we are also offered a token or promise of spirit – a fragment of transcendence.

Some paintings convey emotion more successfully than they convey spirit; others depict the surfaces of life with great realism but have an emptiness at their core. From time to time, however, we come across a work that is almost self-evidently spiritual. Confronted by such a painting, we receive a direct message, unclouded by any differences of intellect or belief or circumstances in life. The artist, in the words of the modernist painter Paul Klee, "does nothing other than gather and pass on what comes to him from the depths. He neither serves nor rules – he transmits." Another pertinent statement on this topic was made by Wassily Kandinsky, who created abstract paintings of tremendous power: in his treatise on art and spirituality, he wrote that "the harmony of colour and forms must be based solely upon the principle of proper contact with the human soul." Art, to be of value, must aspire to the spiritual.

But what of art that has explicitly religious subject matter? Within the Christian tradition artists have attempted to portray spirit since early medieval times. Spend a day in one of the great art gal-

leries and look at the Christian paintings that strike you as being most spiritually profound – works by Giotto, Raphael, Titian or Bronzino, perhaps. In appreciating such art from a non-denominational perspective we do not need to be concerned over much with the literal story that is portrayed. The beauty and truth of a painting – conveyed in the character of the figures, the harmony of the composition, the quality of the light – will carry their own inner conviction into your life.

Another factor at work, no less important, is symbolic resonance. If the work affects you deeply, it could be in part that it works at some archetypal or universal level beyond its precise Christian

significance. Take, for example, an Annunciation scene – the moment at which the Virgin Mary learns from the Archangel Gabriel that she is to bear the Christ-child. Traditionally, such paintings often feature a lily, symbol of the Virgin's purity. A moment of revelation such as this radiates far beyond the narrative. Its universal symbolic meaning is simple but profound: a messenger of the spirit tells an individual that she is to be the bearer of spirit. One does not need to be follow a specifically Christian view of spirituality to feel the deep impact of this idea. Indeed, the critic George Steiner uses the Annunciation as a "shorthand image" for art itself, speaking of " 'terrible beauty' or gravity breaking into the small house of our cautionary being. If we have heard rightly the wing-beat and provocation of that visit, the house is no longer habitable in quite the same way as it was before."

Everything in an art gallery is designed to underline the special status of the paintings inside – the framing, the air of hushed reverence, the formidable guards who keep silent vigil. There are two things wrong with such an atmosphere.

The first problem is that the surroundings, with their obvious symbolism of a cultural treasure trove, get in the way of a true encounter with the content of the work – profound insights passed from one imagination to another. When appreciating a painting, stand or sit comfortably close to it, so that its environs blur into peripheral vision. Observe and acknowledge to yourself the principal content of the work. Let this enter your head without trying to force your appreciation. Do not deliberately think of art in historical or critical jargon. If the painting relates to an imagined scene (rather than being abstract), do not try to visualize it in real terms: accept the painter's rendering. Let your eyes explore every detail of the image; close them for 30 seconds; then open them again, and let the painting flood back into consciousness: you will see it with new understanding.

Great art inspires us by offering glimpses of spiritual truth. Yet to perceive this truth in a museum or art gallery is of limited value, and this is the second problem with the contemporary fashion for treating art as a source of spiritual wisdom (hence the reverential atmosphere). The fact is that we must learn to see our own truth elsewhere, in our own spirit, and live by what we discover. A glimpse, such as art offers, does not generate sufficient light by which to see our way. Even the greatest painting provides merely a window; whereas we must by our own thoughts and actions design, build and inhabit a complete house. In this we are all artists, expressing the ultimate form of creativity. The images by which we live are brushed onto the mind's canvas by the virtues that we direct toward other people.

It is looking at things for a long time that ripens you and gives you a deeper understanding.

·

Vincent van Gogh (1853–90)

exercise 15

the spiritual gallery

Our minds hold a gallery of impressions as rich as any art – including memories of the spirit's purity, consciousness of self, and the qualities that we hold dear. Conjure up an exhibition of your best works, to summarize your creative strengths as an artist of the spirit.

1. Imagine a vast gallery, clean-lined and modern in its architecture. The light of spirit floods in to make this the perfect venue for your exhibition.

2. The works in your exhibition have the following titles: Self, Peace, Happiness, Love, Truth, Forgiveness, Acceptance. Imagine seven blank canvasses hanging on the walls. Their emptiness symbolizes the potential of the spirit, which you have already realized in your own way.

3. Choose an image from life that represents the quality found in each of the titles – perhaps something you have done, said, or thought, or something you are planning. Then, taking each canvas in turn, imagine the paintings coming to life inside their frames, each reflecting your individual style – your creative identity.

4. The exhibition is a retrospective (and prospectus) of your creativity. Dwell on this without pride: all spiritually aware souls discover the creative genius within.

the spirit of music

The anthropologist Claude Lévi-Strauss wrote that "the invention of melody is the supreme mystery of humankind". Of all the arts, music comes closest to expressing the inexpressible. When we close our eyes and listen to a symphony, a string quartet, or a piano sonata, we feel disembodied, as if at last we have been given space for the spirit to unfold. We feel that something (not the composer, not the musicians, but some higher being) is having a spiritual conversation with us.

This idea of spiritual communication is complicated by two aspects of music that belong to a more material realm. 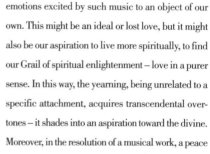 One is its reliance on rhythm, which may ultimately relate to the heartbeat, or to walking, or even marching – a physical dimension most obvious in much modern popular music and some forms of ethnic music. The other is its expression of emotional states. Music of the Romantic age is often experienced as yearning. In the absence of an explicit emotional object, it is possible that we subconsciously attach the

*Just as my fingers
on these keys
Make music, so
the selfsame sounds
On my spirit
make music, too.*

•

*Wallace Stevens
(1879–1955)*

emotions excited by such music to an object of our own. This might be an ideal or lost love, but it might also be our aspiration to live more spiritually, to find our Grail of spiritual enlightenment – love in a purer sense. In this way, the yearning, being unrelated to a specific attachment, acquires transcendental overtones – it shades into an aspiration toward the divine. Moreover, in the resolution of a musical work, a peace will often descend, born out of the initial tensions and contradictions. We may take this as an analogue of our own spiritual journey from confusion to contented acceptance.

Certain types of music lend themselves well to a form of inward reflection – those that are complex and contemplative, such as chamber music and the classical music of North India, played on such stringed instruments as the sitar. The following exercise suggests how to turn a listening exercise into a meditation on the qualities of spirit.

Before you play your chosen music, sit comfortably and close your eyes. Imagine the darkness is the vastness of space, in which the triumph of spirit

will be enacted. Try not to let pictures form in your mind, but instead think of the music as a conversation between your own spiritual qualities. You might experience stringed instruments as love, percussive instruments as strength, piano as creativity, and so on. Any discordant passages might be experienced as spiritual challenges to overcome. Let go of any sense of time. All great music ends with a resolution – a satisfying sense of harmony or loose ends tied together. As this happens, imagine the qualities that you have separately identified flowing back into their source. After the music has ended, sit in silence, aware that the music was not someone else's achievement, but a mirror of sound that reflected your own inner truth.

In Greek mythology, Orpheus charmed the animals with his lyre and voice. Music cannot permanently purify any animal side in our nature, but it can do so for as long as the music plays or lingers in our ears.

inner silence

We live among sounds both pleasing and discordant. We often find ourselves assailed by unwelcome noises from sources over which we have little control – TV and radio trivia from our neighbours, jackhammers in the street, planes buzzing overhead, even the drone of conversations conducted by others. This is why silence is regarded as a positive value. Suddenly we find ourselves alone again, with no unwanted demands on our attention, and it is as if we have stumbled upon a long-lost treasure. Silence is the natural state of the spirit. In its truest form it is found only within, in the core of the self, which is indistinguishable from the spirit. If we know how to access this inner silence, we unfailingly find it, because it is always there, and always has been. To connect with inner silence and to attain spiritual awareness, a true acquaintance with the self, are one and the same thing. How do we penetrate the walls of noise that surround spirit? External noises are relatively easy to avoid, but it is more difficult to muffle the din of ego. Our egotistical attachments, emotions and anxieties create an inner clamour, which we must learn how to quieten. For this, we do not need esoteric, demanding techniques, simply a willingness to listen to the silent symphony of the self, whatever other noises claim our attention both inside and outside the concert hall.

already always

A valuable mantra for meditation would be: *I am imperishable energy, consciousness. I am eternal.* The more we meditate on this acclamation, the easier we will find it to recognize its profound truth. The claims of the material world upon us are, sadly, repetitive. To counterbalance this, a little repetition in favour of the spiritual side of life can do us nothing but good.

In ancient Greece the philosopher Socrates is said to have patiently questioned an uneducated slave boy until the lad revealed that, all his life, he had known a fundamental mathematical theorem, without having been taught it, and without even knowing that he knew it. The truth, said Socrates, is eternal, unchanging and born within us. You need only be reminded where to look, and you will find it lying there in wait for you. We may not accept that scientific expertise is so readily disclosed within ourselves, but certainly that is where to look for truth of the spirit.

One of the reasons that truth may appear so elusive is that most of us, most of the time, are afraid to search. The ego clings to material existence. It insists on its own completeness, its own sufficiency, and turns away from intimations of a timeless inner truth. Locating this truth means clearing away the attachments, desires and anxieties that obscure the purest reality – all forms of psychic clutter that make up the very foundation of the ego.

Purity, peace, love, truth and happiness all lie inside us, ready to be rediscovered. The journey of the spirit concludes at our starting-point. What everyone is looking for is already there, within their grasp, and always has been. We are reminded of the claim made by Michelangelo that his *David*, his *Pietà* and his other great sculptures were already present inside the raw marble blocks hewn from the quarries of Carrara in Italy. He needed to see them there and release them – to actualize their potential. In the same way we can work with what we have to awaken our spiritual qualities. As we energize our capacity to give and to love, as we coax back our inner peace, and as our happiness becomes a daily decision, not a dependency, we realize the true beauty behind the surface of our skin.

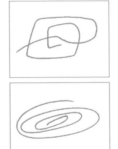

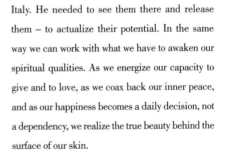

exercise 16

the hidden garden

There are, arguably, five innate spiritual qualities: truth, love, bliss, purity and peace. This exercise helps us to find them within.

1. Picture your inner world as a hidden garden, locked behind ivy-covered walls. Meditation is the key with which to open the gate. Use it to gain entry and look inside. Notice how the flower beds are perfectly tended, despite having been locked away. The patterns they make, the harmony in the colours, seem natural and right. This is your inner truth.

2. Step inside. Your desire to explore, to get closer to the blooms, is the love and acceptance you have for your own nature. Savour it and enjoy the vibrancy of the colours. Feel the bliss that such a sight evokes.

3. Drawing closer, see the completely accepting way that each flower opens, and the perfect ellipse of every petal. This is purity that is never puritanical.

4. Finally, close your eyes and breathe deeply. The scent is overpowering, obliterating any sense of self. This is peace of the soul – undistracted by any clamouring cries of ego.

a quieter world

There is a good reason why many of us spend most of each day distracting ourselves with noise – whether singing or humming to ourselves, chattering to friends, family or colleagues, or leaving a radio or TV switched on. In the heart of silence, our most truthful inner voice can be heard, and we may well be discomforted, even frightened, by what we hear. Yet silence is the natural state of spirit, and we will never connect with its truth unless we can learn to be quiet.

In silence the mind is deprived of one of its major distractions, and hence becomes more reliant upon, more in touch with, its own qualities. The troubled mind will hear the throb of anxieties, and if we are unable to attain self-respect, our sense of personal inadequacy will be deafening. However, the mind at peace will value silence as a clearing in the midst of the world's tangled thickets, a place for contemplating the supremacy of spirit.

If we can come across silent places, in the home or in the garden, or on walks in the countryside, we must be thankful for finding what has become an increasingly rare commodity in our busy world.

To use the gift properly, be still and practise one of the meditations or visualizations in this book. Do not be concerned if occasional sounds interrupt the perfect quiet: think of these as ripples caused by beautiful fish nosing the surface of a still pond. Allow birdsong, whispering breezes and even more discordant sounds such as distant traffic to pass through your mind like the wind in a field of corn.

Some of the oldest meditative practices are accompanied by the sounds of chants or bells. If you opt for this approach to meditation, choose a sound that will fade gently, then ride that sound with your awareness until you find yourself in silence, allowing the calm that is always present within to cradle your inner self. Eventually you will be able to visit this inner citadel of quiet even amid the restlessness of everyday life. Whatever sounds encircle you in the world outside, you will be able to travel, at a moment's notice, to your spiritual place of silence.

exercise 17

the oasis of peace

Peace and quiet exist within all of us, but many of us have lost the knack of finding it. This meditation will help to release it from its inner source, and allow us to rejoin it in our own oasis. Try the exercise in either a quiet or a noisy place: its effects will be the same.

1. Sit comfortably, close your eyes and breathe deeply for a few moments. Visualize that you are sitting alone by the water in an oasis. The desert stretches beyond as far as the eye can see, but immediately in front of you is a fertile haven – your place of silence.

2. Gaze into the mirrored surface of the water. Reflected, you can see clouds passing in front of the sun. These are the thoughts, emotions and memories that prevent you from enjoying your place of silence. Banish the clouds mentally to reveal the unwavering light of the sun.

3. Lean forward and look at your own reflection. The face belongs to a stranger. Is it happy or sad, alert or tired, confident or shy? Does it radiate energy?

4. Now drink from the pool. The water is the pure energy, the silent power at the silent heart of your being. Refreshed, you can re-enter life.

breath of the spirit

From ancient Greece to Native North America, breath has been envisaged as being closely connected with the spirit. Behind much of the symbolism is the notion that breath is a divine gift, returned at death to the donor. In the Hindu tradition of *yoga*, breathing is intended to align individual respiration with the rhythm of the cosmos. Yogis practise *pranayama* (breathing exercises performed through the nose) to strengthen the body, clarify the mind and maintain inner harmony.

There is a direct connection between quality of breathing and inner calm. Anyone who is agitated will experience shallow, fast and irregular breathing; peace of mind is associated with breathing that is deep, slow and regular. Keeping the mind focused by concentrating on breathing is fundamental to some meditation techniques, used to train the mind to be alert and observant. However, not all meditation focuses on breath: this emphasis may be useful, but some of us may find that it encourages excessive consciousness of the body's functions. A troubled spirit will remain troubled no matter how much we work on our breathing. If the idea of breath offers us anything in our spiritual quest, it is as a subject for visualization.

Sit comfortably and take a series of deep breaths. Imagine that you are inhaling truth, insight and pure spiritual energy, and exhaling illusion, egotism and the negative energy of emotions. Visualize the in-breath as blue, and the out-breath as red. At the same time, affirm that spiritual awareness will come as naturally to you as breathing.

Breathing connects us with the whole world, and its history. Someone once calculated that every time we breathe, we are inhaling a thousand million molecules that were exhaled by Leonardo da Vinci (and, of course, Machiavelli and the Borgias). Imagine the infinite exchanges of breath between ourselves and others as an unconscious network of endless giving and receiving, a web of love uniting humanity. In the same way the spirit, which is both individual and universal, participates in a complex system of interconnections. When we feel our breath and contemplate the spirit, we understand our shared humanity with greater insight and truth.

exercise 18

the blissful fisherman

Deep, regular breathing is a tried-and-tested way to generate mental calm. This exercise combines restful breathing with a relaxing visualization that draws upon the age-old symbolism of the nurturing sea.

1. Imagine yourself as a fisherman on a boat in the middle of the ocean. It is a beautiful day; the sun is sparkling on the waves and on the mesh of your net, drifting leeward. Time your breathing to the gentle rocking of the boat as it rises and falls on the ocean swell. Breathe purposefully. Inhale deeply; exhale long and slow.

2. With each inhalation, pull a little more of your net from the water. Although the net is full, you find it easy to haul in, with the swelling waves to help you.

3. Your catch teems with the infinite treasures of spirit: purity, truth, wisdom, patience, love, calm, beauty.

4. As you breathe and pull on the net, you enjoy, in your imagination, the relaxing sounds of the sea and the seabirds all around. You are out of sight of land, but feel wonderfully calm. And you feel your breath as the rhythm of the cosmos itself.

the meditator's path

Meditation is not a difficult or esoteric practice, available only to those of us who are already in touch with our spirituality. Nor is it achievable with only a specific goal in mind. The meditator's path is both endless and endlessly rewarding – an experience of peace, not an act carried out to find peace.

The essence of meditation is a natural experience of healing (the word "meditation" comes from the Latin *mederi*, "to heal"): the call of spirit to the peace within. We all have a need for such healing – if I am honest and look at my own life, I recognize pain, suffering and darkness in certain areas. The deepest repair to our being is when meditation gives us its greatest gift: the realization of who we are. With this comes freedom. The ultimate destination of meditation is freedom for the spirit.

Spirit is distinct from mind, yet may recruit this faculty for its own purposes. Meditation draws these strands together in a unity of being. We are spirit, which is conscious and self-aware; and the mind is our faculty of creation, the canvas on which spirit paints its inspiration to our lives and the method by which we turn that inspiration into a reality. Meditation is the road to self-realization. Along the road we cast aside our many false identities. This is essential if we are to create the internal space in which we welcome back our inner peace.

A common misconception about meditation is that it removes us from consciousness – that we need to stop thinking. In fact, the opposite is true. Meditation teaches us to contemplate ourselves using our purest thoughts (such as, *I am spirit*, and, *My original and eternal nature is peace*). Only thoughts unencumbered by rationalization can open the windows onto self-knowledge and self-understanding.

As our spiritual self-awareness becomes stronger, so does our ability to move about in the world as free and assured human beings, with increasing calm amid life's turbulence. We also gain a greater capacity for empathy and compassion toward others who are not at peace. Meditation gives us a sense of the togetherness of all things – the community of spirit. We are able to appreciate each of our worldly experiences with a more focused vision of what is important.

A simple exercise demonstrates the capacity of meditation for revealing what is true. Bring to mind your name, but do not associate it with yourself. Hold the image of its letters in your mind and speak it silently to yourself. What does it mean? Does it connect with your identity? Many people, when they do this exercise, find that the thought of their name out of context is quite bizarre. By focusing their mind fully on the essence of the word, they experience a fundamental (if not profound) truth: our name has no essential meaning or importance and no true relation to who we are, it is merely a practical convenience.

Its reality is not self but sound, an articulation of the tongue experienced by the ear; or a pattern of signs, selected from the repertoire of the alphabet. It floats in the mind like a spacecraft from an alien planet.

If this truth is available by such a simple meditation, imagine the scope for insight when we begin to meditate on whole thoughts, experiences or actions. Inevitably, as horizons open up to us by expanding spiritual awareness, we will more keenly sense suffering and evil in the world, as well as beauty and goodness. Try not to let this deter you from your path. Simply try to acknowledge any unhappiness as the way life is at the moment. This serene acceptance opens us to a spiritual opportunity: the chance to let the light of our inner peace shine through the compassion we can create for all that is suffering as much as it shines in the joy we have for all that is good. If we can prevent ourselves from identifying with all that appears as sorrow and pain, we can deepen our perception to give us a greater connection with life. This is meditation of the most practical kind.

When we begin meditation it is often best to find a quiet, empty space, with few distractions (perhaps a room in your home rarely visited by others), in which to learn to focus our minds. Start with ten or fifteen minutes per day. You might lengthen this if it seems appropriate after your initial sessions. Soft lighting can help the atmosphere. It is also worth trying a guided commentary to start with – a recording by an experienced meditator who can lead you into soul-consciousness. At the end of the session, reflect on your experience, and note how your mood is changed, and how valuable the meditation has been.

We might use a mandala (a geometric diagram) or a mantra (a chant) to help us become more conscious of ourselves as spirit. We can create our own mandalas from nature – perhaps the head of a flower, or the veins on a leaf. Spend time looking at the pattern before you. Try not to stare but allow your focus to rest gently. If your object is, say, a flower, every aspect has an equivalent within spirit: think of the flowering of spirit, the emergence of its full fragrance, its perfection, and so on. A mantra can be any spiritual insight that empowers and calms us, such as *I am spirit* or *I am peace*. Simply repeat the phrase to yourself, silently if you prefer, and let it fill your consciousness.

The deepest, most empowering form of meditation, however, is that which focuses on the self as spirit without any external aids. The self is experienced as a point of radiant spiritual light. Or we simply savour the quality of our own peaceful thoughts. In this gentle but self-illuminating focus, we can truly experience ourselves and become the master of every thought and action. Our inner peace radiates from deep within through everything we do and say, permeating all our interactions. Meditation at this level expands and maintains self-awareness, and restores self-sovereignty. It creates a peaceful and loving mind, reaches the still, silent core of the self, and opens that silence to divine power, to be touched, taught and transformed. Light enters and opens the spirit.

exercise 19

inward signposts

Below are two approaches to meditation, one based on visualization, the other, more advanced, on pure thought.

the river

Visualize yourself walking along a river the length of its journey, from a noisy, crashing mountain stream, to a broad, deep meander where only a floating twig or two reveals its movement, and finally to the meeting with the ocean, where all is still, silent and peaceful. This is what I experience inside. Calm, quiet, stillness.

the self

In the purest form of meditation you take yourself as your object. A simple idea – such as, I am a peaceful soul – comes to life as you experience it. There is no deliberate repetition, only a stream of thoughts – the right kinds of thoughts, based on an understanding of self as spirit. It does not matter how fast the thoughts flow, so long as they are moving. If they wander, gently bring them back. In time they will slow down, and you will be able to savour them. They flow from the eternal empowering qualities of purity, peace, love, truth and happiness within yourself. In pure self-realization, you experience yourself as radiant light.

yoga and the art of union

When most of us hear the word *yoga*, our minds conjure up images of contorted postures accessible only to the extremely agile. However, as with meditation, there is nothing essentially complicated or mysterious about yoga. Its simplest definition is "union". If we bear this meaning in mind, we will see that we spend large amounts of our lives "in yoga" – even over the course of a day we move from one union (interaction) to another. These are the temporary unions of our consciousness – with objects, ideas or other people. They tend to be brief, mental attempts to unite with something outside ourselves, and while this has little to do with spirit (and more to do with desire and attachment), it does demonstrate our natural inclination toward unity.

In the East, ancient yoga traditions have detailed architectures on how to build our lives around a yogic path. Breathing techniques, *asanas* (postures), purification and detachment all comprise the language of the yogic journey.

The goal is to achieve direct union with the (divine) source, so that we may be purified and liberated from our worldly trials and even, as some believe, our worldly existence. But to achieve this union we need not feel that we have to make a long and arduous inner journey, crossing stages of painful sacrifice and initiation as we graduate from one level of enlightenment to the next.

Ways have been developed that enable us to touch the light much faster than we might by more ancient methods. While our awareness of the source might dim so as to be lost in the darkest corner of our consciousness, our eternal connection with it is as imperishable as the spirit itself. In fact it can take only a second to reinvigorate the communication between the heart of our soul and the heart of the divinity. This is the essence of yoga – a love-link with the One who never stops loving. But it does require three things: the realization that we are eternal spirit; the recognition that we have a parent spirit,

> *As the waters of the Ganges flow incessantly toward the ocean, so do the minds of the bhakta [yogi] move constantly toward Me, the Supreme Person residing in every heart, when they hear about My qualities.*
>
> •
>
> Bhagavata Purana
> (*c*.500BC)

with whom we have a unique personal relationship; and (perhaps the most challenging step of all) the suspension of our attachment to the material world of objects, ideas – and people.

However, we need not wait until we have completed all three steps, in whole or in part, to begin our journey of yoga. The postures of mind and intellect are more important than postures of the body. A healthy relationship is built, sustained and matured in the exchanges of open, honest and intimate communication. Our relationship with the source is no different, except that it is silent.

To prepare ourselves for this conversation with the source, we must ensure that we have the correct state of consciousness. We release our awareness of worldly distractions, dive deep within ourselves and become conscious of our spiritual identity. Once we

have realized our inner peace, through meditation, we can turn toward the source and open ourselves to transmit and receive the pure light of love. We will know that we have achieved union when our transmission is returned through waves of love penetrating our being, in the same way that the sun's warmth penetrates our skin. We will be aware of the most subtle of beings shining benevolence across our spiritual path in rays of light. These are like seeds planted in the soul which burst forth in our intellects unexpectedly, to empower us and lighten our way in a world of many falsehoods. They serve to remind us that we have achieved yoga and that we are now living in the light of our parent, friend and guide, the source of love, truth and power – now only a moment away. This living remembrance is yoga of the most natural kind.

prayer and affirmation

Throughout the world, ritualized devotion is the most popular way to make contact with the divine. It can become as automatic or mechanical as our acceptance of a doctor's prescription; moreover, it can block out awareness of the devotee's own greatness of spirit. Yet ritual arguably serves the desire to acknowledge truths in actions untainted by worldly significance, and in this sense is consistent with spiritual awareness. Those who subscribe to particular religions will have strong views about their motivation for worship and its practice. Others whose faith is personal may want to adapt their own rituals. Others again may want to retain traditional, ancient rituals.

Within a non-denominational way of life, ritual's meaning becomes personalized. Bowing down in devotion may seem problematic for those who believe that the spirit lies within, but even that time-honoured form of worship could be treated as a self-ennobling act, in the way that a citizen bows down to receive the sword of knighthood.

However, prayer, within institutionalized religions, is often an expression of wishfulness, hope or fear. How do we explain that someone can pray for peace, then half an hour later become angry? The answer is that prayer cannot transform spirit. It can meet various needs that people, in their religions, have felt over millennia. For example, prayer formalizes a perceived relationship between the individual and divinity; it expresses a longing for a better world; it invokes the name of God to bring blessings. But without spiritual awareness, prayer and other forms of institutional worship are like houses without roofs. They are ill-equipped to serve the principal purpose for which they are intended: bringing the divine into our lives.

For many people on the road to spiritual awareness, affirmations will be more appropriate than prayer. These are formal statements, intense with conviction, self-belief and determination. An example might be: *I am love. My purpose is to give love.* The avowal is made with such conviction that it becomes a performative statement, like *I swear* in court, or *I do* in marriage: it has the force of an action. Affirmations attract their own truth. We express what we believe, and the belief becomes concentrated and self-evident. By these quintessential truths we sustain ourselves on our journey.

exercise 20

safety from the flood

Religions can be institutionalized, but spirit cannot. Learn to recognize the personal truth that you can find in various forms of worship, and let that inform your own realization of self as spirit.

1. In your imagination, visit as many places of worship as you can, covering as many faiths as possible, while observances are being performed. You empathize with the worshippers and recognize the strength of faith and commitment that each individual shares with you. Meditate on your connections with these people: you are all essentially spiritual beings.

2. Imagine your thoughts riding a vessel, carried along a powerful river, which is the strength of your own spirit. Rain falls for many days and a flood rises, obscuring the shape of the river, but you are safe in your self-belief. You invite the worshippers from each faith, each group on its own separate mountain, to board your ship. In time the flood rises above the mountain tops.

3. Safe in the ship, meditate together and feel the sense of community. The rain stops and the waters subside. The land appears again, so your guests happily leave the vessel. You feel a deep connection with humanity.

on retreat

The journey to inner peace is an ongoing process of rediscovery conducted within the context of everyday life. To arrive at our destination, we do not need to become monkishly ascetic and isolate ourselves from society, neither must we rise at five and live on a frugal diet. However, periods of retreat – a weekend, a week, even longer if possible – can certainly help us to tap deeper into our inner silence, and in this respect a brief retirement from the distractions of daily living can benefit everyone.

First, the act of going on retreat affirms our commitment to spiritual priorities. We undertake, as a conscious act of maintenance and renovation, to allow our spirit to nurture us while banishing the most obvious contrary pressures.

Secondly, we give ourselves time – or more strictly we remove ourselves from time. For as long as we are on retreat, our lives cease to be governed by the anxieties of clock time. If we are on communal retreat, we might, of course, observe regular times for meals and shared meditation or other group activities. The clock we follow on communal retreat is an aspect of our respect for others, our readiness to accept the collective qualities of spirit, the bonds of joyful responsibility that we share with our fellow retirees. An essential part of being on retreat is aloneness, amid an atmosphere of quiet, and this is the third and most important benefit. When we are alone and silent, the conditions are exactly right for us to renew the most intimate knowledge of ourselves, to delve deep into the core of spirit, and perceive, with modest gratitude, our innermost qualities of purity, peace, love, truth and happiness.

Meditations performed on retreat are particularly rewarding. We begin to feel that we are making the right internal connections once again, and we feel ourselves becoming stronger, more self-sufficient, and more able to give to others. Any temptations we might have felt fall back into perspective, as unworthy and harmful distractions to our true purpose in life: they lose their lustre and wither in our hearts.

Organized retreats are increasingly popular, and the settings for such organized sessions are often beautiful in a way that can help to promote tranquillity. Certainly, a degree of silence is necessary for a refreshing retreat, and this is often found in rural surroundings. However, the company is more important than the aesthetics of the place. We might look forward to arriving at a hilltop hideaway or wooded paradise; but if we can arrange to be among spiritually aware souls, sharing each other's silence and energy, honouring each other's individuality, we can come closer to the spirit of the thing.

A retreat, like a meditation, can take place anywhere. You can even go on retreat in your own home, if you are able to be mostly silent for a day or so. You might decide to ignore the phone during the day, then pick up messages in the evening – or leave them until the end of the retreat. You might rise early for a dawn meditation. The fruits of retreat, organized or private, lie within reach of us all. In harvesting them, we are reminded of the most valuable truths of the spirit, we are refreshed by all-enveloping calm, and we are energized in our spiritual growth for the future.

sleep and spirit

According to the neuroscientist Allan Hobson, the mind is sometimes externally orientated (while awake), sometimes oblivious (during sleep) and sometimes "so remarkably aware of itself [during dreams] that it recreates the external world in its own image." Others go even further, claiming that "wakefulness is nothing other than a dreamlike state", modified by input from the external world. This is why we talk about spiritual "awakening": the life we lead in the physical world has dreamlike unreality, not least because we eventually emerge from it into the more lasting reality of eternity.

For centuries, dreams have been invested with spiritual importance as a source of prophecy, visions, insights, and visitations from the divine. Carl Jung believed that interpreting dreams for their symbolic meanings could lead to the discovery of a repressed religious instinct in the dreamer – a longing for spirituality stemming from the collective unconscious, the pool

And if tonight my soul may find her peace in sleep, and sink in good oblivion, and in the morning wake like a new-opened flower, then I have been dipped again in God, and new-created.

·

D. H. Lawrence
(1885–1930)

of our deepest, most time-honoured intuitions. In dreams we might occasionally encounter an archetype (universal image) known by Jung as the Wise Old Man, who might appear as someone we know or as a stranger. Look out for such elderly, authoritative figures in your dreams and heed their messages, bearing in mind that you may have to use inspired guesswork to arrive at an interpretation. Dreams of infinity, or flight, or dazzling illumination, can also have a spiritual meaning: if these dreams have a mood of elation, treat them as reservoirs of spiritual power revealed within yourself, and try to tap this power in your meditations.

Dream interpretation does not suit everyone, but undoubtedly fascinating themes for contemplation and analysis can be generated when our dreamlife is subjected to scrutiny. Even though the meanings we impose may not have been "intended" by the dreaming mind, there can be value and truth in self-analysis that uses dreams as raw

material. What we are really asking is: *If this dream is meaningful, what meaning is consistent with the most important truths we know about ourselves?* Those who find dreamwork rewarding can proceed from dream interpretation to lucid dreaming, a set of techniques that give the dreamer the power to make conscious decisions while dreaming (say, choosing a path at a crossroads), while retaining some elements of surprise. People who have mastered lucid dreaming say that they gain a sense of peace and focus in their waking lives, too. Taking some command over dreams may be valuable practice for learning to control the everyday delusions,

attachments and pointless fears that may inhibit spiritual growth.

But let us return for a moment to the notion of sleep as an unenlightened state. In *Hamlet*, Shakespeare wrote: "For some must watch, while some must sleep; thus runs the world away." But proverbs often refer to habit, and we have seen that habits are seductively comforting attachments that prevent us from realizing our full potential. We all have the capacity to watch rather than sleep, to awaken to the reality of spirit (who we are) and offer our energizing power to all those who slumber around us.

energies of love

Our lives are webbed with interactions. We start as babies with fundamental needs that our parents satisfy. From that point on our relationships become increasingly complicated. Emotional neediness continues to grip us, causing tensions and fault lines even in bonds with friends or workmates. But if we can gain true self-respect from the knowledge of our own limitless value, we can move away from dependency to a more open, giving approach to others. In the process we live happier lives. Rediscovering our spiritual awareness transforms not only our relationships with family, friends and acquaintances, but also our encounters with strangers. When we walk into a room full of people, every stranger has unique gifts, which may be offered or withheld. An unspoken empathy connects everyone present in a limitless potential for love and happiness. If we are truly enlightened, we let our own gifts overflow so that everyone with whom we come into contact benefits equally from our energies. Even troubled souls who resist our overtures will be touched by the light of our radiance. By awakening to spirit, we banish fear from our transactions with others and admit love in its place. No one can truly hurt us, whatever we do. By extending forgiveness to those who treat us less than respectfully, we accumulate the spiritual credit of karma. We are blessed in proportion to what we give.

the art of selflessness

The most obvious meaning of selflessness is denial of one's own comfort, convenience, materialistic wealth, and other benefits, for the sake of others. By extension the word has come to mean a generosity of spirit so great that we put other people's interests before our own. An archetypal figure of selflessness would be Mother Teresa of Calcutta, whose work led to her being canonized as a modern-day saint. If we choose to live by the spirit in everyday life, a degree of selflessness is inescapable.

What is the source of selflessness? The answer to this question is the process described elsewhere in this book, in which a profound love for the self as spirit spills over into love for humanity, until this endless donation of our energy becomes a crucial part of our purpose and meaning in life. In time selflessness becomes a reflex, so that we reach out a helping hand even before we have had time to think about it. Our reaction is not something that we learn by precept but an intuition that we rediscover inside ourselves. It lies latent in everyone, as we often find at the scene of an accident. True, there will probably be morbid voyeurs, but there will also be helpers, who put themselves at personal risk to give assistance. On the whole, the instinct is alive and well, and part of our responsibility as spiritual discoverers is to ensure that its channels are open so that selflessness is automatic.

There are certain practical measures we can follow to ensure that we may be of service when required. Learning first aid is an obvious example. Add to this a further seven measures of your own devising and resolve to put at least one of the eight into action now. You will never resent time spent on others, because you will know that there can be no better way to spend time. How far should we go? None of us needs to aspire to sainthood, because we define ourselves negatively when comparing ourselves to an ideal. We cannot have an image of selflessness, nor a timetable for attaining it. Self-sacrifice might be measured in terms of what we relinquish. Yet, selflessness as an aspect of spiritual awareness involves no sacrifice. It is the opposite: a wonderful enrichment of the self, prioritizing what we give over what we take.

exercise 21

learning to give

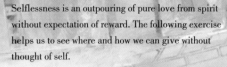

Selflessness is an outpouring of pure love from spirit without expectation of reward. The following exercise helps us to see where and how we can give without thought of self.

1. Choose a seat on a busy street and watch the passers-by. What do you see? An older woman struggling with her shopping bags? A child in distress? A homeless person begging for money or attention? Think about what you could give to ease their pain.

2. Put your ideas into action. Use your intellect and the power of spirit to make life better and easier for others. Help a frail person across the street. Make time for a friend in need. Smile at someone who is down on their luck, hear what they have to say and find a way to make a difference – buy them a sandwich or bring a blanket the next time you pass. Offer help spontaneously and try not to consider the time it takes to give.

3. Take your meditative mind with you wherever you go. Be observant and aware of all that is happening around you as it takes place. Open your eyes to everything and be fully engaged in all of your activities. When you see with open eyes, your heart will open too.

through fear to love

The Greeks spoke of *agape*, the love for humankind. The love that flows from us in all directions, embracing strangers as well as friends, family and acquaintances, is the highest love of all, and the truest expression of the spirit. However, many people seek, for various reasons, a special, companionable, usually sexual relationship with one other person. Although we do not have to live within a couple in order to achieve fulfilment, it is true that a special partnership of this kind can be an enlarging experience, provided that certain emotional hurdles can be overcome.

All too often love is the thing that we are looking for above all else, the universal grail we think will change our life. We see it as the virtuous recognition by another person of our own intrinsic worth. Yet what is the torch that we use as we stumble around in the dark in search of this elusive gift? The answer is: need. We take our need on a foray into the world and try to match it to an object that fits its shape precisely. We might dress up this quest in

Love is an image of God, and not a lifeless image, but the living essence of the all-divine nature which beams full of all goodness.

•

Martin Luther (1483–1546)

different terms, insisting that we have so much love to give. Yet the truth is often more raw and more poignant: what we have is a huge, naked emotional need for love, and a fear of remaining in this state of unsatisfied longing. In our quest to fulfil our need, we are prepared to delude ourselves with unsuitable partners.

Most schools of psychoanalysis would contend that the love we seek as adults is an echo of the love we sought as children from our parents. Many therapists would point out that the tensions and anxieties associated with our adult relationships – in particular, the fear of love being withheld – reflect our childhood insecurities with regard to one parent or another. According to this psychocentric view of life, mature relationships are marked by emotional needs and dependencies that derive from childhood's emotional scars. Many adults allow the love of another person to define their being to such an extent that, if and when they are rejected, they lose all sense of who they are,

what their purpose in life might be. Even if the couple stays together, the relationship is marked, on one side or both, by fear. Spiritual awareness is the process of moving from fear to a richer, more tolerant, more relaxed form of love.

Love as an emotion brings people together prematurely and convinces them that they can live together. If the relationship develops badly, resentment and jealousy can set in, which is unsurprising, given the emotional roots of the attraction. Then the relationship may founder painfully, and one or both partners may find it difficult to have faith in love again. Alternatively,

the bond may solidify into permanence, in which case the inevitable rifts and tensions are simply delayed. Like earth tremors along a fault line, they tend to break out, causing harm.

However, there is another possible course for emotional love to follow, and that is to blossom into true love as the initial heat of emotions cools down and a wiser, more mature perception takes its place. True love requires a cool climate. This is not to say that there is no room here for physical contact, only that the full onslaught of passion is destructive if it is the basic foundation of intimacy.

As we have seen, love in its pure form is an upwelling from the depths of the inner self. It is a radiance that the energized, self-aware spirit scatters in all directions, like the seed from the bottomless bag of a tireless sower. This is done in a spirit of courage. The more timid way is to hoard all our seed for our own purposes, or to offer it to a few chosen intimates who can be guaranteed to be grateful for our gift and to allow the seed to germinate.

Although the height of spiritual development is to love humanity as a whole, many of us have or seek a special relationship that is exclusive with regard to sex and, to some degree, to regular companionship. Mature love for a partner involves body, heart and mind together, but at a deeper level this will also be an act of spirit. We enter a conscious recognition of, and commitment to, another self who is distinct and independent, yet at the same time shares with us a spiritual affinity, a two-way current of openness and empathy that gives both parties enlarged possibilities for fulfilment. We need not expect love to be easy – growth rarely is. Opening up in a special way to another spirit may result in all kinds of inner shifts and shuffles as our centre of gravity adjusts to new circumstances.

Many people in love make the mistake of narrowing their perspective on the world, rather than taking the opportunity to broaden one's horizons. The result is that if the relationship should happen to come to an end, two people are left impoverished rather than enriched, as they face the prospect of falling back upon reduced resources. However, when love is pure, the end of a relationship leaves us undamaged. This is not to say that the experience will be painless, simply that there is no need to fear the pain. We can still move confidently forward in the knowledge that our well of love will never dry up, even though there may be a temporary blockage in the supply.

Love consists not of gazing at each other in a swoon of dependency but of looking both inwards and outwards, sharing each other's insights and also the larger love – *agape* – for all our fellows. To sustain such a relationship requires openness and independence of spirit. As the great wit Dorothy Parker said, "Love is like quicksilver in the hand. Leave the fingers open and it stays. Clutch it, and it darts away."

exercise 22

the enchanted forest

Love in the commonly understood sense can be overpowering and mysterious. But, to an enlightened being, love is neither. This visualization prepares you for your progress from worldly to spiritual love.

1. Imagine yourself in a dark forest at night. If you like, make it an enchanted, fairytale wood, from your childhood memories.

2. Picture yourself stumbling through the undergrowth, branches catching in your hair and roots tripping you as you walk forward. All around there are unidentifiable rustlings, and the muffled sound of wings passing overhead. You can't remember how you arrived in the forest, or how to get out.

3. Suddenly you realize that you can see colours. The sun is coming up. Imagine how brilliantly green the leaves look in the first light of day. As light fills the forest, you realize that it is not at all densely wooded. You are in a glade, and there is another glade nearby. You can rest or explore. There are paths if you want to leave, but you no longer feel any need. You have found love and its infinite life-enhancing beauty. You are ready to give love wherever you go.

passion and enthusiasm

Many words related to mind and spirit carry multiple meanings and, of these, few are more confusing than "passion".

The difficulty arises from the use of the word in different contexts to indicate intensity of emotion, all-absorbing sexuality, and strength of belief. One meaning can shade into another. Some people hold an idea so tenaciously that they feel a stirring of emotions whenever they speak about their belief, or whenever they hear it contradicted. This flies in the face of spiritual awareness, which involves detachment – an unshakeable conviction in spiritual truth that has no roots in the soil of the emotions, but thrives in the pure air of intellect. We may say, colloquially, that we are passionate to discover the truth; but as soon as we feel this mission excite emotions, we know that it is time to take stock of ourselves. Emotions in the service of truth are still emotions, and can be dangerous dust storms that veil the truth in a cloud of ego.

We all know the traditional image of the holy man or woman as an ascetic figure, withdrawn from the world and dutifully, dispassionately pursuing a life of wisdom and good works. This idea is often extended to other vocational truth-seekers, such as philosophers and scientists. Yet, as a student of genius once pointed out, people like Sir Isaac Newton, who discovered the laws of gravity and made many other important contributions to science, did not toil over a problem for hour after hour from a sense of duty. They did it from a sense of joy, because the problem fascinated them and filled them with excitement.

For those of us trying to explore the nature of the spirit – just as surely as a scientist does when he tries to fathom the workings of nature – discipline and singlemind-edness will only take us so far. Discipline can, dangerously, become a goal in itself, and an addictive source of pride. We are pleased with the hours or the effort we are putting in, and forget what should flow from them. And so, gradually, we become more and more obsessed with our own capacity for work, and ignore the fact that truly creative leaps of the spirit are

made in a state more akin to play. The ancient Greeks believed in *enthousiasmos* – from which we derive the word "enthusiasm" – which marked the moment when divinity poured into the selfless void. The enthusiast was, literally, someone who acquired godlike powers.

Even in the stark, no-nonsense workplaces of the modern world, we sometimes receive intimations of this divine force. All of us, at some time, when we are truly enthused by some project, experience tirelessness, a feeling of exhilaration, as if energy is flowing into us from some deep inner spring.

Enthusiasm – like joy – is infectious. We radiate it back into the world, for others to pick up and use. If we are living by the light of the spirit, the energy that we give out will take the form of enthusiasm for all the things about which we feel positive. And, while our intellect will remain unclouded, dispassionate, we will, at the same time, feel joy as we pursue our highest priorities in life.

It is possible to feel clearly as well as to see clearly, and as we travel on the road to spiritual awareness we will one day live the truth of this optimum balance.

empathy and understanding

It has been said that no spirit heals alone – we grow by and through other people. There is a Hebrew phrase for this: *Tikkun Olan*, the collective spiritual effort to heal the world.

Opening ourselves to those around us is a vital aspect of spiritual growth. Think of it as being a blossoming, which takes place only as the sun of spiritual strength begins to climb towards its midsummer zenith. Spiritual peace gives us the ability to connect with the souls of others – to know intuitively their experiences without being consumed by them.

Those without peace tend to veer between two extremes. On one hand, we are like detuned radios, deafened by the static of our own thoughts and emotions and unable to pick up outside signals accurately. On the other hand, without our own spiritual core acting as an inner compass, constantly restoring our equilibrium, we are vulnerable to being swept away by others' energy, in the form of intense emotional need or focused will.

When one of his monks recently returned from 17 years in captivity, the Dalai Lama asked him if there was any moment during that time in which he felt himself to be in danger. The monk paused for a moment. Then he replied that there *was* one moment when he was aware of great danger, and that was when he nearly lost his compassion for his captors.

It is in the marriage of empathy and understanding that compassion is born. This is one of the purest faces of our spiritual potential, and it lifts us above the urge to judge others, which we know has its foundation in our own insecurities. Compassion is the first ray of light we can give those who are obviously in the dark. In this way we begin to fulfil our spiritual destiny and our duty to enlighten our fellow travellers.

Attentiveness and openness are two of the most important qualities in developing a feel for, and understanding of, other people. There are a number

*If you want others
to be happy,
practise compassion.
If you want to
be happy,
practise compassion.*

•

Dalai Lama

(b. 1935)

of exercises that we can do to improve these attributes in ourselves.

The first of these exercises involves choosing an acquaintance, or someone you have read about in magazines or newspapers. Hold in your mind the image of what they do for a living. Then think of all the positive qualities they must have to do their jobs properly. Imagine them at work showing these qualities in action.

For the second exercise, you will need a large piece of paper and a pen or pencil. Draw a circle and in the centre write the first name of someone you know. Randomly around the circumference of the circle draw small blobs here and there, to signify the specific emotions and attachments to which this person is prone. Now draw a larger circle around the whole. Imagine that the central circle is a sun and draw its beams as they radiate to the outer circle – the edge of the universe. The blobs of emotion and attachment block some but not all of the rays. The essential qualities of the spirit shine through. To complete your spiritual diagram, make a list of these qualities as they appear in this specific individual, along the rays that you have drawn.

karma

Karma is the law of returns, the system around which the spiritual universe is organized. It is a system of natural justice whose outcome is based not on moral judgment but on the principle that what happens to us – what we receive – automatically reflects what we do, what we put in. All karma comes from the quality of our consciousness. Karma is internal, occurring within the spirit.

This can be understood at various levels. At the most basic, we can find out for ourselves how giving brings immediate benefits: it makes us happy. On the other hand, when we take, when the ego controls our motives, we become spiritually tense. This is karma at its most immediate.

At another level, we can think of karma as a complex network of spiritual cause and effect in which we place our trust. Everything returns to its own state of balance. If we live well, in peace and love for others, without thought of material gain, our spiritual enrichment will inevitably travel back to us, perhaps

Nothing can have as its destination anything other than its origin.

•

Simone Weil
(1909–43)

along circuitous paths. We may not see the immediate effects of living in this way, but they will inevitably return to us and enrich our spirit by accumulation. In this way we are thoroughly in control of our destiny.

At a more profound level still, many people believe that karma and reincarnation are inextricably linked. This enables us to understand the differences in fortune that we experience in our lives on Earth – some rich, some impoverished, some at peace, some at war, and so on.

The mystical implications of this are complex, but it may help to think of reincarnation as an allegorical rationalization of the physical laws of cause and effect. Our previous lives should not be visualized literally; material concepts cannot describe the ineffable.

Karma is to do with the quality of living. If we are to practise karma at the most elevated level, we must live by what we experience in our hearts rather than merely doing good by following precepts. You can give a person a meal every day, and keep them alive. But it is preferable to

teach them how to fish and cook for themselves, because then they are free and independent. To teach somebody about karma and how it works is ultimately to free that soul from what they have done in the past, and make it possible for them to create their own future.

Some people who know a little about karma focus on what they see as its dark side: punishment for past actions, a retribution that will eventually catch up with us. In fact, if there is punishment at all, it is self-punishment. An action that is carried out in the wrong state of consciousness results in our feeling pain, at a spiritual, mental or emotional level. This, in the terms of a more judgmental ethical system, is "sin". But, in fact, while karma is an immutable law, our very understanding of it liberates us and encourages us to live joyfully. Once we recognize karma as the universal system of natural justice, we are freed from the burden of being the judge and jailer of other people. Moreover, karma encourages and empowers us to give the deepest joy from our heart today, knowing that such radiance will reflect back on us tomorrow.

family and spirit

Our family relationships are a lens that throws into high magnification how we feel about each other. Emotions often seem more intense in a family context. Family members have an uncanny and unerring ability to zero in on our insecurities: they know the buttons to press to bring a rush of emotion.

Often they oscillate violently between extremes – anger melting into reconciliation which in turn shades back into anger; or jealousy turning full circle into pleas for forgiveness.

This volatility can be explained by a number of factors. The first of these is the physical closeness that family relationships entail. When we share a roof, or make regular visits, we cannot so easily put problems on hold. The second reason is the accumulated history that makes family relationships so complicated. The phases we've gone through, the intimate knowledge we share, the great intimacy that inspires contradictory feelings of jealousy, closeness, irritation and an overwhelming need for approval – all create a complicated setting for the quest for spiritual awareness.

It is commonplace to think of the family as a wellspring of values – such as love, generosity, loyalty, truth – that have strong spiritual overtones. Indeed, family values rank high in a number of religions, including Christianity, Judaism and Islam. Confucianism also places great emphasis on filial piety, the respect, love and duty due to one's parents. But, in fact, the family is best thought of as an environment that poses spiritual challenges.

Families are often held together by ties of emotional needs, and these are inimical to the true expression of the spirit. The basic challenge for anyone whose life is strongly coloured by the family (that is, most of us) is to reconcile family responsibilities and sensitivities with the development of the spirit, which must lift itself above this level of emotional insecurity to breathe freely. What does this mean in more concrete terms? To breathe freely is to lose emotional dependence, which in no sense means an end to responsibility, or caring, or loving. Self-respect is at the core of spiritual life and self-respect is impossible without

knowing that one has fulfilled one's obligations. We must decide what value we place on support for our relatives, both junior and senior. We may find ourselves with many dilemmas – for example, should we modify our own goals to spend time with a lonely relative? Such questions should be seen against an understanding of our overall purpose in life: to give love. The answer to this particular dilemma will depend on circumstances (as we evaluate them) and on our own instinctive assessment of what feels right. We should look out for the ego's tricks: if we believe that a parent or uncle or aunt must get used to being alone, is this an impartial judgment, or is it ego using plausible excuses for self-interest?

One of the great privileges of being alive is the contact we have with the young – whether our own family or the children of friends. In having children ourselves and bringing them up inspiringly, we send gift-wrapped messages to the future, influenced by our spiritual example. Yet we can also learn from children. It is not that they are spiritually aware, although the myth of child-like innocence is proving difficult to dispel. More accurately, we can say that there is much to be learned from the speed at which they themselves learn, their intuitive insights, their intolerance of jargon, bluster and social refinement, their enthusiasm for discovery. Anyone involved in childcare would do well to bear in mind the wise words of Carl Jung: "If there is anything we wish to change in the child, we should first examine it and see whether it is not something that could better be changed in ourselves."

friendship and spirit

A friendship is an elective kinship – a conscious commitment to sharing a line of supportive or enjoyable communication, and keeping that line open. For many, the value of friendship goes beyond company, exchange of ideas, shared activities. Friends can enjoy a communion of spirit in a purer, less complicated sense than is readily attainable between sexual partners.

For the Greek philosopher Epicurus, friendship was crucially important because it both built upon and transcended the principle of utility (usefulness, pragmatism). "To eat and drink without a friend," he wrote, "is to devour like the lion and the wolf." From an origin of utility comes love, and the loving friend is urged to be courageous, even to die for his companion. In classical myth, such friendships often became passionate. In the Trojan war, Achilles responded to the death of his friend Patroclus by smearing dirt on his head and hands and writing on the ground in a paroxysm of grief – an extreme example of friendship acquiring an emotional charge that brings turbulence to the spirit when external circumstances sever or otherwise damage an attachment.

Yet the Epicurean emphasis on courage can be extended to have special relevance for modern friendship. To show love to a friend, and perform acts of selflessness on his or her behalf, requires courage in a society suspicious of altruism. We need more courage still when we project love toward the fringes of our acquaintance. The truth is that spiritual kinship is present in all our relationships, because spirit is the universal source of self, the wellspring of energy that all individuals share. In this context, courage is self-knowledge and acceptance, bringing the confidence to give, to allow friendship to become the basis of all our approaches to other people.

If we are spiritually aware, our friendship will radiate toward everyone we meet. No rebuff will be able to hurt it.

Friendship runs dancing through the world bringing to all of us the summons to wake and sing its praises.

·

Epicurus
(341–270 BC)

exercise 23

circles of love

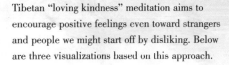

Tibetan "loving kindness" meditation aims to
encourage positive feelings even toward strangers
and people we might start off by disliking. Below
are three visualizations based on this approach.

1. *List a close friend's five most valuable qualities.*
Imagine each as stemming from a single source, like
tributaries from a pure spring in the mountains. This
source is spirit. Trace the tributaries to the source.
Let the imagery fade, but continue to contemplate
the meaning that underlies it. The mountain is just
a pathway, enabling us to apprehend pure spirit.

2. *Repeat the exercise with a less close friend. Then,*
dwell on the feelings that you have for both friends.
You know one better, but your feelings about each,
at the spiritual level, are the same. There is no
correlation between intimacy and value. Every
friendship is precious beyond comparison.

3. *Build on this exercise to include people whom*
you dislike initially. Contemplate their positive
qualities. These people too are fed by the spring of
pure spirit. Feel your reactions to them becoming
more positive.

forgiveness and reconciliation

The degree to which we can forgive people is the degree to which we love them. When our hearts are hardened against others, we draw in the pain of any hurt that they have caused (or that we imagine they have caused), and this pain festers deep inside us, creating darkness and poison. Forgiveness is the natural state of the spirit, an aspect of spiritual health, a petal on the flower of love. Resentment is an illness of the spirit, which sabotages our peace of mind.

Anyone who wishes us harm is emitting a powerful and misdirected energy, which is rooted in their own pain and anger. They are in fact wishing harm upon themselves. When we forgive, we send out healing, loving energy and lift their negative feelings a little, casting a ray of light into their hearts. That ray reflects back to us and we become stronger. At the conscious level, the ray may be denied by the person who has felt its touch. However, it is certain that its influence has been absorbed. No gift of positive energy will be totally declined by the recipient: some of the energy will always be used, adding to the world's sum of goodness.

When a mother forgives the tantrums of her toddler, or the rebellious anger of a teenage son or daughter, it is because she knows that her child is innocent. The spirit is learning, struggling against the grip of the ego. We are all surrounded by innocent souls who have lost their shine, dulled by neglect, tarnished by the acid of the ego. When a friend lashes out unexpectedly at us, we catch a glimpse of a soul that needs to be reached. Sending back to that friend a message of acceptance and love, we transmit positive energy. We inspire peace.

We can choose our feelings. When we are ridiculed for an opinion, or badmouthed by a colleague at work, or someone barges into us in their thoughtless haste, it is sometimes difficult to prevent a surge of turbulent reaction. But once we have stilled the destructive emotional wave, we can opt for the path of forgiveness. This is essentially an inner gesture of acceptance, a refusal to deny this person the warmth that we radiate toward everyone else. In practical terms we might choose, after such an incident, to acknowledge and contemplate for a few minutes one

of their virtues, as a sign of our spiritual kinship with them. Even if we do not know the person well, even if we would not choose to spend time in their company, it is good practice to dwell on their qualities in this way.

Forgiveness is a declaration of the heart, backed up by a resolution of the mind. We may wish to devise some kind of visualization or outward gesture to mark our inward gesture of blessing – perhaps a putting together of hands, imagined or real. Performed as a true act of spirit, forgiveness takes a moment. Realistically, however, many people are first going to endure a period of coming to terms with the issue, before concluding that forgiveness is the only possible solution.

A colloquial expression for forgiving somebody, or making up after a quarrel, is "burying the hatchet". The instrument of aggression is laid to rest. However, from this expression a modern proverb has emerged: "It is one thing to bury the hatchet, another thing to forget where you have buried it." One temptation might be to accompany forgiveness with pride in one's own tolerance and charity. This engenders a false virtue. True forgiveness involves a complete levelling of the score, an acceptance of equality with the forgiven party, a refusal to dwell on either the fault that has supposedly been committed or one's own effort of absolution.

None of this means that we must cease, at the practical level, to stand up for ourselves. If someone tells lies about us, forgiveness does not require that we leave slanders uncorrected; if someone conspires to cheat us out of our inheritance, we should write letters and consult a lawyer, if we wish to. The important thing is to follow such a course of action in a spirit of constructive redress. In our hearts the only battles we have to fight are against our own worst instincts.

a world without strangers

Atmosphere means "sphere around the soul". We create our own atmosphere and, if we are spiritually aware, it is charged with positive energy that reverberates all around us. This is the subtle touch of love that may help to waken others from their habitual slumber.

People who are not fully awake tend to build up walls that define and segregate their lives from others – like hibernating animals cocooned in their protective dens. But what happens when we reach beyond the barriers to make connections with people – not just our friends, work colleagues, and acquaintances, but also strangers, with whom we might come into contact just once in a lifetime?

Spirit binds all humanity into a profound kinship. We are all equal in having the same qualities of spirit and in our potential for love, courage, patience, trust, honesty and forgiveness. Yet as individuals we often tend to arrange people in a hierarchy of intimacy which

Do not neglect to show hospitality to strangers, for by doing that some have entertained angels without knowing it.

·

Hebrews 13:2

puts strangers beyo
for the victims of wa
but the majority of
daily li
in coun
to us, a
what th
as a blu
imagina
ening to
what, e
do for t
and blo
It is
that ov
kindnes
suspici
have b
that peo
from th
spiritual journey b
one, and a natural c
approach strangers
Imagine that you are
cuss some non-cont

of their virtues, as a sign of our spiritual kinship with them. Even if we do not know the person well, even if we would not choose to spend time in their company, it is good practice to dwell on their qualities in this way.

Forgiveness is a declaration of the heart, backed up by a resolution of the mind. We may wish to devise some kind of visualization or outward gesture to mark our inward gesture of blessing – perhaps a putting together of hands, imagined or real. Performed as a true act of spirit, forgiveness takes a moment. Realistically, however, many people are first going to endure a period of coming to terms with the issue, before concluding that forgiveness is the only possible solution.

A colloquial expression for forgiving somebody, or making up after a quarrel, is "burying the hatchet". The instrument of aggression is laid to rest. However, from this expression a modern proverb has emerged: "It is one thing to bury the hatchet, another thing to forget where you have buried it." One temptation might be to accompany forgiveness with pride in one's own tolerance and charity. This engenders a false virtue. True forgiveness involves a complete levelling of the score, an acceptance of equality with the forgiven party, a refusal to dwell on either the fault that has supposedly been committed or one's own effort of absolution.

None of this means that we must cease, at the practical level, to stand up for ourselves. If someone tells lies about us, forgiveness does not require that we leave slanders uncorrected; if someone conspires to cheat us out of our inheritance, we should write letters and consult a lawyer, if we wish to. The important thing is to follow such a course of action in a spirit of constructive redress. In our hearts the only battles we have to fight are against our own worst instincts.

a world without strangers

Atmosphere means "sphere around the soul". We create our own atmosphere and, if we are spiritually aware, it is charged with positive energy that reverberates all around us. This is the subtle touch of love that may help to waken others from their habitual slumber.

People who are not fully awake tend to build up walls that define and segregate their lives from others – like hibernating animals cocooned in their protective dens. But what happens when we reach beyond the barriers to make connections with people – not just our friends, work colleagues, and acquaintances, but also strangers, with whom we might come into contact just once in a lifetime?

Spirit binds all humanity into a profound kinship. We are all equal in having the same qualities of spirit and in our potential for love, courage, patience, trust, honesty and forgiveness. Yet as individuals we often tend to arrange people in a hierarchy of intimacy which

Do not neglect to show hospitality to strangers, for by doing that some have entertained angels without knowing it.

•

Hebrews 13:2

puts strangers beyond the pale. We might feel for the victims of war or famine or earthquake, but the majority of people we encounter in our daily lives (many more in city than in country, of course) mean nothing to us, and we may not even register what they look like. To see people as a blur in this way is a failure of imagination and of spirit. By awakening to the reality of others, and to what, even in a small way, we can do for them, we enlarge ourselves and blossom into wholeness.

It is not uncommon to believe that overt acts of friendliness or kindness to strangers will provoke suspicion or even fear. Many of us have been conditioned to accept that people do not want to be stirred from their reveries. However, the spiritual journey brings us closer to everyone, and a natural corollary of awareness is to approach strangers with openness and love. Imagine that you are meeting a stranger, to discuss some non-controversial matter, or even a

controversial one. Why not take along a gift? If you spend an hour or so together, why not treat this as quality time, to learn from and teach a fellow spirit, in a process of mutual enrichment?

The *sarangi*, a musical instrument of the Indian sub-continent, has "sympathetic strings", whose function is to vibrate in sympathy with the strings plucked by the musician. When we offer love to a stranger, their sympathetic strings vibrate in harmony with ours. Even when we seem to be rebuffed, which happens occasionally, there is no doubt that the positive energy we have emitted will strike a hidden chord of peace.

Meditate on the web of connections that link us to everyone else in the world. Think for a few minutes of all the people who invisibly touch your life every day. Let your spirit emanate light to change the vibrations around you. Open yourself to allow the positive energies of others to flow with your own.

Watch a stranger going by. Watch how they live their life, their expressions, their postures, the way they present themselves to the world – try to grasp an idea of the true self within from their face and behaviour. At all times, be mindful of the value of others.

inner strength

The self-evident truths about life are the ones that we neglect at our peril: we will all encounter misfortune; we will all die. Spiritual awareness gives us the strength to come to terms with circumstances when chance sabotages our expectations, when we lose cherished friends, or when we face the unknown ourselves – the new adventure for the soul that has reached the end of its earthly sojourn.

We often pursue our course in life without thinking about chance and mortality, and how these factors impact upon our understanding of identity and purpose. To sidestep these issues is dangerous, leaving us limited resources for dealing with the unexpected. If we discover the truth of the spirit, we will see the whole of our physical life on this planet in a new perspective that gives us strength to weather the storms. We learn, through self-exploration, that the spirit thrives in a dimension altogether distinct from that of the body. The pain we feel when plans fall through, or when our best friend dies before us, is the pain of attachment, which can be reduced by prioritizing elsewhere. Through detachment, we can even find strategies for managing pain.

Inner strength is available to us all if spirituality wins the battle against egotism. All around we find inspiring examples – people who show immense courage in the face of hardship, whose spirit shines through with glints of humour. By making spirit our priority, we will have access to a reservoir of strength when the time comes.

living with loss

Death, in all cultures, is formalized: there are prescribed modes of grief, age-old rites of burial and cremation. In the West there is also a vast literature of consolation, recognizing that the loss of a friend, relative or partner is traumatic. For survivors, the spirit becomes turbulent, as we try to rationalize bereavement. Mourning is the permission given by society for this disruption to take place.

The word "loss" is accurately connected with death: in mourning, I represent my own point of view. It is as if a part of me has died, because I have welcomed you to live in me. Often, mixed with sadness, there is also guilt that I did not value you enough.

Sadness and guilt are both illusory if we can reach an understanding of our place in the spiritual framework. As beings of spirit we are indestructible. At death, we return "home", to the source – which Christian consolatory imagery sees as the bosom of the Lord. Alternatively, it could be the beginning of a new adventure: rebirth. These images help to portray the spirit's departure from its spent body. Spiritually, life holds no loss, only movement. Guilt is unhelpful, as it mires us in the past. Sadness is unhelpful, as it too energizes attachment to the past. The present and future are where we fulfil our potential for love.

Yet what am I to do with my sadness, which mingles personal loss with the sense of wasted opportunity, the frustrated potential of the deceased to spread love and happiness? In eradicating emotions of loss, we may feel that we are undervaluing a life, concentrating on our own viewpoint and failing sufficiently to honour the contribution made by the friend, relative or lover whom we have lost. The answer is to find a way to commemorate without attachment. We will find our own way to do this, and we may even borrow the traditional formalities of remembrance – the photo album, the pilgrimage to meaningful places – to honour the intrinsic value and beauty of another soul, whose new adventure is just beginning.

I think that the dying pray at the last not "please", but "thank you", as a guest thanks his host at the door.

•

Annie Dillard

(b. 1945)

exercise 24

a ship sails away

Grief can be so intense that any consolation may
seem like a candle taken on a night walk through
a jungle. Yet the bereaved can take great comfort in
words. This exercise begins with a quotation from
Victor Hugo's *Toilers of the Sea*, which someone drew
to my attention after my mother died. Read the
quotation, visualize the image, then offer your blessing.

the image
*"A ship sails and I stand watching until she fades on the
horizon and somone at my side says, 'She is gone.' Gone
where? Gone from my side, that is all; she is just as large
as when I saw her. The diminished size, and total loss of
sight, are in me, not in her. And just at the moment when
someone at my side says, 'She is gone,' there are others
who are watching her coming, and other voices take up
the glad shout. 'There she comes!' And that is dying."*

the blessing
*The death of the loved one is a time to offer him or her
blessings for their journey, and an invocation of joy as
they sail over our horizon toward the beyond. By
holding on, we subtly hold back: so let go. Offer your
joyful blessing and imagine it attended by the affirming
cry of seabirds and the soothing rhythm of the waves.*

beyond pain

After years of sickness and unhappiness, the German philosopher Friedrich Nieztsche had an important spiritual insight: in a moment of elation he realized that all his suffering had contributed to what he was, and to the possibility of experiencing such a blissful moment. He decided then that a truly enlightened consciousness was one that could say "Yes" to its whole existence, and would choose to repeat that existence in exactly the same way, given the chance.

A number of esoteric traditions teach that pain is something the spirit chooses in order to temper itself, like a blade on an anvil. The task is not to conquer pain, but to discover what it can teach us. For the development of the spirit, it is said, a change in consciousness is more important than a cure. Some mystics deliberately inflict pain on themselves as a way of denying the body and bringing themselves closer to God.

There is a sense in which pain exists only in the mind. According to the respected "gate control" theory, various parts of the nervous system are responsible for different parts of the experience of pain. The spinal cord registers shock, one part of the brain analyzes the nature of the hurt, another part produces a sensation of intense discomfort. There are psychological techniques to turn off this last experience (including hypnosis) – that is, to remain aware of the pain without experiencing its unpleasantness. Like all negative energies, pain can be acknowledged and accepted, then released. This is similar to the way in which we can deal with our emotions (see p. 71), not by fighting them, but by detaching ourselves from them.

We might create in our minds the image of a room in which we carry out all our mental and physical functions. The lamp in this room is the spirit. Within the room we consciously place the pain in a cupboard and close the door securely. The pain is still there, but it is shut away from the spirit, the essential experience of the self's identity. If we give spirit our attention, our bodies will be bathed in its pure light, and the pain will be experienced and accepted on the periphery of our being instead of in the centre, leaving the mind able to continue its functions.

exercise 25

mastering the dragon

Many people, distracted by pain, find relaxation – and thus meditation – impossible. This exercise provides a way of managing pain by using the experience itself as the subject of a meditation.

1. Your pain is the easiest thing to concentrate on, so use it as the focus of meditation. Begin by describing it to yourself as fully as possible. Where is it? Is it stabbing, or dull? Is it hot? If so, is it like the heat of a poker or the heat of spreading wax?

2. Form a mental picture of your pain, based on your description. You might imagine it as a piece of music played by an orchestra, or an oil slick on the sea, or as the movement of a machine, such as a clock or a set of gears. Concentrate totally on the pain, and whenever it varies, however slightly, vary the image.

3. Take slow, deep breaths. As you exhale, imagine the image changing as a little of the pain leaves you. When you inhale, bring the pain back. This may seem odd, but you are learning to control it. It will be slightly smaller each time you recall it. You will not erase the pain all at once, but you can ease it by degrees. Eventually, it will be significantly reduced.

life's trajectories

An air stewardess, scheduled to work on a particular plane, for some reason had her duties re-organized and was no longer required on that flight. The plane crashed with the loss of many lives. Her narrow escape was traumatic for her. Under counselling, she felt that she had to do something completely different to help her mind recover, something connected with nature. So she travelled to a wildlife camp in Uganda, to observe mountain gorillas. One day rebels attacked the camp and she was taken hostage. The hostages were divided into two groups. She was in the group that was released; the rest were murdered.

Chance can lead us into extremities – situations far removed from those to which we have become accustomed. Or at a more mundane level, chance can spoil our plans and appear to sabotage our hopes. When such eventualities arise, our capacity to sustain peace and contentment independently from the ebb and flow of life's incidental circumstances can be severely tested. Yet the infinite network of cause and effect, seemingly random when seen from an individual viewpoint, is inevitable when looked at in a sufficiently global perspective. This is the environment in which spirit exists – the backcloth against which our life unfolds.

To be spiritually aware is to understand that chance is not a lottery, it is a system, an environment. To an enlightened person, there are no accidents or coincidences. At a profound level we can see this system as karmic – the events that befall us can be read, literally or symbolically, as the consequences of past actions, possibly in previous lives. Here, though, we are more concerned with the shallower dimension of the present. At this level chance manifests itself in the material world, not in the spirit. Spirit animates our physical form, and as beings of spirit we shape events and take responsibility for them.

The choices we make radiate outwards into the world of phenomena. This is why to a truly enlightened soul there is no such thing as chance. In many ways we are saying this when we discuss karma. Every effect has a cause, and the original cause of everything is spirit (downward causation). What appears to be chance is simply your karma returning.

Think of a share-dealer on Wall Street who does voluntary social work among New York's poorest communities in his spare time. In his profession he may accumulate wealth to start with, then suffer a reversal, and end up in debt. To other people, he may appear to be a failure, and perhaps attract some disgrace. But, ultimately, what does this matter if he has slowly and steadily been accumulating spiritual wealth through selflessness? Weighed against the spirit, material well-being does not even register on the scale.

When we realize ourselves as spiritual beings, we learn that our lives are in one sense determined, yet in another sense we enjoy free will. Actions that start with the highest qualities of spirit are able to exert an influence, which operates at a level where chance can do no damage. We are free, because we are not attached to a material agenda. Our detached involvement in the world is our guarantee that the network of cause and effect can never become our enemy. If we radiate love, we will be without enemies – we are safe.

journey's end

West and East have different ideas about aging. In the West, after retiring from work, we tend to potter about gently until we die. In the East, old age is the time of wisdom and spiritual energy, when we are most equipped to give to others the benefit of our experience. We would do well to absorb the lessons of the East, replacing the all-too-common sense of gradual decline with a more accurate realization of the potential that remains to us still, long after our physical powers have started to weaken. Our body may lose its lustre as we age, but experience can burnish our spirit to a gleam that is ever more radiant.

We all have to face the reality of death, but the closer we move toward spiritual awareness, the less significant this moment will seem. In any case, we have probably noticed how elderly people seldom speak of death as fearful – perhaps after so many decades on the planet some spiritual awareness is absorbed into even the most materialistic of life's pilgrims.

For us to exit the physical body painlessly, we may choose our own moment of dying. This is known as

"dying alive" – the conscious choice to acknowledge and let go of everything to which we are attached. Death is painful only when we cling to attachments while at the same time being wrenched away from them. Think instead of death as a gliding return to home – gradual, inevitable, flawless, natural, the spirit's ascent to its resting place, regardless of whatever is happening within our body at this time.

Death is frequently depicted not as a homecoming but as a shadow, a bruise on our daylight. But imagine trying to run away from your shadow: you will never succeed in shaking off this persistent companion, however fast you run, and you will exhaust yourself in the process.

However, as an alternative scenario, imagine yourself walking contentedly into the shade cast by a large tree. Your shadow will disappear, and your eyes will adjust to the reduced levels of light. You will be able to see no less clearly. Fear of death, like fear of spiders or mice, comes not from the nature of things, but from an illusion that lodges persistently in the mind.

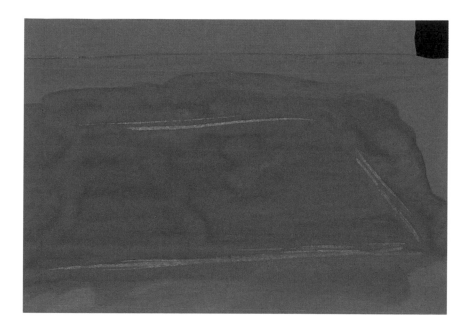

In modern life (and especially in working life), we are programmed to believe that time is precious in itself – one of the reasons why death can so easily come to be seen as a threat. We think of ourselves, misguidedly, as citadels under siege, knowing that we cannot hold out: we must give up our treasures to the enemy. Misconceptions about time also explain why so many people are unprepared for retirement – the sudden change from famine to abundance is experienced as psychic shock. But in fact if we think of time as simply the medium in which we regain spiritual awareness, the road along which we travel for a while, then at journey's end we will not feel the loss of any commodity. We might savour our memories, but not with pangs of severance. We are returning to the source, laden with spiritual riches in joyful abundance.

The realization of our spiritual identity brings with it eternity and freedom from fear. We will die alive, liberated in life. We are fully prepared to move on to a new adventure, as effortlessly as moving from our living room to our bedroom at the end of the day.

conclusion: *a new way of grace*

Early on in this book we started to think of the spiritual quest as a journey, which could be completed at any time, unexpectedly, in a split-second, once we set out on our inward road to awareness. By now we will have understood that reaching awareness is the beginning of a further journey, which might be described as the journey of the aware spirit through our own life and the lives of others, and ultimately through and beyond our own death. It is on this journey that we acquire our most profound and mature character as a unique source of peace and love in the world. The growth and change that affect any child who passes through puberty and adolescence into adulthood are as nothing compared with this growth and change toward spiritual maturity. We never cease to learn, and because our motivation is love, which touches the vital lives of others, much of what we learn gives us joy – we receive from others the sparks of their inner light, ignited by the light that we cast upon them.

We probably know a few people who have something of this character and maturity, and no doubt we admire the way in which they carry themselves through life. Such people have a magnetism. They are endlessly giving and caring, and full of laughter and wisdom that seem to be reflections of each other. They always seem able to say the right thing for the circumstances, and even when they make mistakes, and are embarrassed for a few minutes, they seem never to lose their true sense of who they are. Their actions and words strike us as the natural unfolding of the best that lies within their spirit. We see no division, no public self and private self, or different selves for different company. Somehow, spending time with such a person seems a privilege to us. The more we get to know them, and learn of the life-problems they have had to contend with, the more we love them.

Spiritual awareness is the secret such people possess, and it has become *our* secret – a tremendous gift that we have rediscovered, within ourselves, for which we feel eternally grateful. There is an old-fashioned word, "grace", which deserves to be rehabilitated as a description of how we behave, how we appear to the

world, when we have come into possession of this gift. The word implies a rightness of thought and action, and a beauty that stems from this rightness. This beauty is far from physical, but it makes an immediate, inspiring impression on all those who come into contact with it. It is the spiritual life made manifest in day-to-day speech and behaviour. It is an authority worn lightly, a strength that runs deep but is never solemn or stern. Grace is the way we live when we are spiritually aware and are building upon that awareness in all our transactions with the world.

Once acquired, grace becomes ingrained within us. After we have discovered our true self, the truth of the spirit, we have no wish to return to the divisions and tensions of unawareness. This does not mean, of course, that we are completely immune from the temptations of attachment, the lure of the comfort zone, the stirrings of emotion. For a moment we might be unsettled, we wobble, muster the strength to right ourselves, and continue on our way. We know that attachment, comfort, emotion are false friends, and that the cost of following them, the loss – even temporarily – of the wonderful gift that we have acquired, is insupportable. Spiritual awareness, once attained, has a self-correcting mechanism. Resisting the sideways pull of material attachments, we continue on our true course.

It is important to remember that the attachments of the material world have outposts in the spiritual world. That is, our knowledge of the spirit can become a source of pride; our habit of meditation can become a comfort zone. These are the points at which we might lose the grace we had acquired. But if our self-understanding is sure, we will recognize these pitfalls intuitively, and stay away from them. If we live by the revelations of spirit, we will be invulnerable to error.

The highest spiritual work is a lifetime vocation, and lies well beyond the scope of this book. However, even within the framework of less rigorous aims, each day is a chapter on our own spiritual journey, each relationship a chance to love a kindred spirit, each moment pregnant with profound choices – all impacting on our private and public destinies. As all the great teachers of wisdom advised, we must also be vigilant and guard the gates of our new-found truths against the invaders of illusion – for there are those around us

still who prefer to remain asleep, to be the same as they have always seemed to be, because they are not yet ready to let spirit shine. We must do our inner work quietly and deeply with an aura of humility – respecting all who come in curiosity to knock at our life's door. We all have our purpose to fulfil, and if we follow that purpose with steadfast dignity and grace, others will borrow the light that we generate to illuminate their own way. Indeed, we must consciously direct this light for their benefit – like a traveller at night who shines back his or her torch to ensure that those behind can pick their way over the same difficult path.

A life of spiritual awareness is the life for which all the ingredients of the inner and outer universe are designed. All other ways of life are aberrations, which carry a high cost to the individual – high levels of stress and weak resources to cope with illness, bereavement and the prospect of our own death. All around us we see people who are prepared to shoulder this burden without complaint. But we have only to walk among them, as ourselves, to shed light for them to live by if they choose. Through our radiant spirit, we increase the sum of love and peace in the world.

A noiseless patient spider,
I mark'd where on a little promontory it stood isolated,
Mark'd how to explore the vacant vast surrounding,
It launched forth, filament, filament, filament, out of itself,
Ever unreeling them, ever tirelessly speeding them.

And you O my soul where you stand,
Surrounded, detached, in measureless oceans of space,
Ceaselessly musing, venturing, throwing, seeking the spheres to connect them,
Till the bridge you will need be form'd, till the ductile anchor hold,
Till the gossamer thread you fling catch somewhere, O my soul.

.

Walt Whitman
(1819–92)

bibliography

*The following is a list of
books on related topics.*

Dowrick, S.
    Intimacy and Solitude, The Woman's
    Press Ltd, London, 1992

Dreher, D.
    The Tao of Inner Peace (new edition),
    Penguin Books, London and New
    York, 2000

Dyer, W. W.
    Wisdom of the Ages, HarperCollins,
    London and New York, 1998

Evola, J.
    The Doctrine of Awakening, Inner
    Traditions International, Rochester,
    Vermont, 1996

Gawain, S.
    Creative Visualization, New World
    Library, Novato, California, 2002

George, M.
    In the Light of Meditation, O Books,
    Ropley, Hampshire, 2004
    Learn to Relax, Duncan Baird
    Publishers, London, 1998; and
    Chronicle Books, San Francisco, 1997

Hansen, C.
    *The Tao Te Ching on the Art of
    Harmony*, Duncan Baird Publishers,
    London and New York, 2009

Katagiri, D.
    Returning to Silence, Random House,
    New York, 1988

Kriyananda, S.
    Awaken to Superconsciousness, Crystal
    Clarity Publishers, California, 2009

Macdonnell, M. et al.
    The Path to Inner Harmony,
    Southwater, London, 2008

Nelsen, J.
    Serenity, Conari Press, Berkeley,
    California, 2008

Smullyan, R.
    The Tao is Silent, HarperCollins,
    London and New York, 1977

Thurman, R.
    Inner Revolution, Random House,
    London and New York, 1999

Walsh, R.
    The World of Shamanism, Llewellyn
    Publications, Woodbury, Minnesota,
    2007

Weiss, B.
    *Eliminating Stress, Finding Inner
    Peace*, Hay House, London, 2003

Wilkinson, T.
    Lost Art of Being Happy, Findhorn
    Press, Findhorn, Scotland, 2007

Wilson, P.
    The Quiet, Macmillan, London, 2007

index

encounters, exchange of
energy 27, 32–33, 34
energy *see* spiritual energy
enthusiasm 127
Epicurus, on friendship
134
existence
philosophies of 16, 18, 25
self and 24
see also identity

F

family, and spiritual life
132–33
fear, and self-knowledge 33
feelings 26–27
sensitivity and 27
flowers, and meditation 43,
44
flowing uphill, Daoist exercise
79
forgiveness 136–37
free will, and determinism
147
freedom, and responsibility
58–59
friendship 134, *135*
fruits, meditations on 46,
47

G

Gandhi, Mahatma, on reason
24
gardens 83
Gawain and the Green Knight,
self-examination and 48

Gibran, Kahlil, on winter
48
Giotto, art of 93
God, ideas of 36, 38–39
Gogh, Vincent van, on art 94
grace, and spiritual awareness
150–52
Gyan, pillar of spiritual life
20

H

Hamlet (Shakespeare) 117
healing, spiritual 34, 106
Heidelberg University,
philosophy walks 46
Heraclitus, on change 30
Hinduism
material perception and
18
the *sri yantra* 44
Hobbes, Thomas, on human
nature 56
on reason 24
Hobson, Allan, on the mind
116
honesty, toward self and others
64–65
Hugo, Victor, on death 143
human nature 56
Hume, David, view of the
self 54
humility, ego and 62–63

I

identity 50, 52, *53*, 111
uniqueness of 56–57

see also existence
illness, and energy flows *35*
imagination 16, 22, 80, 84
visual 92–94, *95*
see also visualization
inner silence 98–117
intellect 27, 54, 55
intuition, reason and 24–25

J

James, William, on theory of
emotions 71
jealousy 26
journal, stream of
consciousness and *23*
Jung, Carl, on dreams 116
on children 133

K

Kandinsky, Wassily, on art
92
karma 34, 130–31
chance and 146–47
Klee, Paul, on art 92
Kubler-Ross, Elisabeth, on
self and others 32

L

Lao Zi, the *Dao De Jing* 76
Lawrence, D. H., on sleep and
spirit 116
Lévi-Strausse, Claude, on
music 96
life
cycle of life and death 46,
89

Further Information

For further information on any of the ideas or exercises in this book, you can contact Mike George by e-mail at: mike@relax7.com

Acknowledgments

The publishers would like to thank the following people for permission to reproduce their artworks.

Marion Deuchars

pp. 15; 22; 28; 36; 40; 44; 50; 61; 66; 77; 81; 99; 117; 118; 141; 149

Joelle Nelson

pp. 27; 31; 43; 57; 59; 63; 65; 69; 74; 83; 97; 111; 115; 129; 131; 133; 138; 150; 153

Aud Van Ryn

pp. 18; 25; 33; 49; 55; 71; 82; 89; 91; 93; 102; 107; 123; 127; 137; 142; 144

Every effort has been made to credit copyright holders correctly. We should like to apologize for any errors or omissions, which we will endeavour to rectify in future editions of this book.